Here's Erma!

Here's Erma!
The Bombecking of America
by Norman King

Caroline House Publishers, Inc.
Aurora, Illinois

10 9 8 7 6 5 4 3 2 1

Copyright © 1982 by Norman King

Copies of this book may be purchased from the publisher for $8.95.
All inquiries and catalog requests should be addressed to Caroline
House Publishers, Inc., 920 West Industrial Drive, Aurora, IL 60506.
(312) 897-2050.

ISBN: 0-89803-050-1

Library of Congress Cataloging in Publication Data

King, Norman, 1926-
Here's Erma!

   1. Bombeck, Erma—Biography. 2. Authors,
American—20th century—Biography. I. Title.
PS3552.059Z75 814'.54 [B] 81-10054
ISBN 0-89803-050-1 AACR2

Contents

Chapter 1

Roots

Humor Is a Full-Time Job

The woman is pleasant-looking, housewifey, brown-eyed, and comfortable. She speaks in a mild middle-American voice, usually accompanying her speech with a smile. Her words may be mild, but occasionally they carry hidden barbs.

It is morning, seven-thirty by the block, and the woman sits at a typewriter in a garage that has been converted into a workroom at the back of a suburban house in Paradise Valley, Arizona.

After a long time cogitating, she finally inserts a blank sheet of typing paper into the typewriter and stares at the paper. Her mind runs down a long list of ideas she has been mulling over in her mind. In despair she discards every one of them.

She glances around at the walls of her workroom. Pages of feature articles, framed and mounted, hang on the walls. One of the pictures is entitled, "The Socrates of the Ironing Board." It is a photograph of her, the likeness unmistakable. There are Headliner of the Year awards and photographs of friends, among them Dinah Shore, Arthur Godfrey, Paul Newman, and Art Buchwald.

1

There is more. One visitor described the interior decor as part Mexican, part Indian, and part Early American, plus. Plus what? The woman remembers that her visitor asked her, with slightly subdued malice, "Do you do your own decorating?"

"Me a decorator?" she replied. "You're kidding. I'm terrible. I should be put in a burlesque house. I could do a terrific job. I like bright colors and all kinds of wild stuff."

She glances at the clock. Somehow a half hour has slipped by. She hasn't got a word on paper. Is it time to panic? Why not? It's always time to panic. Maybe today is the day her inspiration dries up. Maybe today is the day she loses the formula. Maybe today is the end.

In her mind she dies. She dies a lot, like a heroine in the movies. In her mind she sinks slowly to the floor. She pulls all sorts of faces, dying dramatically, dying gruesomely, dying gracefully.

Writer's block, she thinks. I've caught writer's block.

But then, she thinks that every morning when she sits down to write. And, after all, what is writer's block but insecurity? And what is insecurity but the very essence of her writing? In every word she writes, her insecurity shows. It is her style, her message, her tone.

What to write? Today there's nothing.

She remembers Ernest Hemingway's words of advice about writing: "Get it down first, and then get it right."

So she types. "I'm a real recipe freak."

But that isn't right. Too flat. Too obvious. And it isn't really her. That's getting it down, as Hemingway says, but not getting it right.

She starts in again.

"This is probably going to blow my image, but I'm a real recipe freak. I read cookbooks like other women read erotic novels, English mysteries, or humor."

She smiles. That's a neat touch, people reading humor. Wishful thinking, maybe.

Her fingers fly now, and she's into it.

"Because I am a student of cookbooks, I have developed some insights over the years . . . especially with a section that has become a staple called 'Celebrity Recipes.'"

And that's the theme of the piece.

It's easy sailing now.

"But mostly, I'm suspicious of them. Like Angie Dickinson's date and nut bread. The picture above it shows Angie with her long blonde hair falling over her shoulders, wearing a see-through net dress that hugs her bones. I'm sorry, but I somehow get the feeling if someone offered Angie a measuring cup, she'd laugh and say, 'I haven't worn that size since I was seven.'"

And she goes on. "Barbara Walters' cabbage rolls seem out of character somehow . . . nor do I figure Menachem Begin sitting around in Israel one afternoon announcing, 'We got any cinnamon? My mouth's just watering for some of my apple pancakes.'"

Within twenty minutes she's flying.

"Every time I see one of Jacqueline Kennedy Onassis' recipes, I know it's going to require béchamel sauce and it's just as well you don't make it because you wouldn't be able to pronounce it if someone asked you what you served.

"Same thing with Princess Grace, who always shows off and gives her recipes in metrics. (How soon they forget Philadelphia.)"

And by now, of course, it's obvious that the woman at the typewriter is none other than humorist Erma Bombeck, newspaper columnist syndicated in over eight hundred papers, magazine contributor, book author, lecturer, and television humorist—the woman who single-handedly has brought the art of newspaper humor into the age of women's liberation without sacrificing any of its bite, its wit, or its special pain.

Bombeck's efforts appear to be effortless musings, ramblings more or less off the top of the head—things you might hear at a cocktail party or over a cup of coffee in a suburban kitchen.

That's what they are *intended* to be.

But the appearance is deceiving. Anyone who has tried to write anything—even straight expository stuff—knows that the most difficult material to write is humor.

At the same time it is the most rewarding. Not only does someone laugh at your musings, but you are usually well paid for your work.

Bombeck herself once observed with some sardonic humor:

"I get letters from women saying they'd like to write a column because they have four hours of free time now that the kids are in school, and they really could use the money. Oh, boy! They don't realize it's a full-time job that requires total discipline.

"And you know what my discipline stems from, don't you? Insecurity. In every word I write, it shows. You're just basically so afraid that someone's going to find you out. Somebody's going to say, 'That's not such a big deal, what she does. Anybody could do that.' "

Anybody?

Let anybody try it.

Actually, under the deceptive cover of ease and facility, the humor columnist in America today typically has devoted years of struggle and anguish to developing his or her art.

Bombeck is exceptional because she is a woman, writing about women's frustrations and headaches in a land still basically and essentially male-oriented and macho-skewed.

Let's look at a bit of history.

Laughing at Life in Ohio

Erma Bombeck was born on February 21, 1927, in Dayton, Ohio. She was the daughter of Erma Haines and Cassius Fiste. The name on her birth certificate was Erma Louise Fiste.

"I don't know if people are born with a sense of humor or develop it for some particular reason," Bombeck says, reminiscing on her origins, "but mine had been there for a long time. My family laughed a lot, and maybe that rubs off."

Well, they laughed *sometimes*, anyway, according to her mother's recollections. "Sometimes when she said something she thought was funny, I'd just lie back and let her have it," says her mother, who was then Mrs. Erma Fiste and is now Mrs. Erma Harris.

Someone once asked Erma Harris if she herself had a sense of humor, and the story goes that she pointed to her daughter and said: "I had her, didn't I?" At least, that's the way Bombeck tells it.

The Fistes were not what could be called a well-read family.

"My dad was a laborer," Bombeck recalls. "I come from a whole line of laborers and Ohio farmers." She had never lived on a farm, but she had the proper farm background. Like many women in farm and labor families, her mother had gone to school only through the fourth grade.

But her mother thought she could see a marvelous career in the future for her daughter. A movie fan, she loved screen kids like Shirley Temple and Mickey Rooney.

"I was a stage mother," Erma Harris admits. "I pushed Erma up front. When she was about four, I started her out in singing and dancing. She was a blues singer and she won contests."

Bombeck remembers it all with some sad resignation. "My mother wanted me to sing and dance my way out of poverty, like Shirley Temple. It didn't matter that I had no talent and that my hips were saddle bags; I had to go to dancing school."

Her mother didn't really understand that she had no interest in dancing and singing. She wanted to write. "I never thought about a writing career," her mother admits.

In the long run, all the dance routines and the singing auditions came to nothing. Bombeck suffered the exercises and the shape-ups, and her teachers suffered along with her. It never took hold.

Many years later, when she eventually made guest appearances as Erma Bombeck on television talk shows, her mother finally changed her mind about journalism.

"Mom still isn't impressed by the writing part of my job," Bombeck points out. "But when I go on TV, she's happy. She thinks, 'Erma finally made it in show business.'"

When Erma Fiste was nine her father died. "Mother was twenty-five," Bombeck says, "and after his death she got a job in a General Motors factory in Dayton."

Mrs. Fiste worked there as a "stator winder."

"I never really knew what she did," Bombeck confesses. "I never knew what a stator was." In fact, she still doesn't.

This all happened in the depths of the Great Depression, a very bad time for a mother and her child to be left alone by the death of the man of the house. Bombeck and her mother were forced to seek shelter at her grandmother's house.

Erma Fiste's way of life altered radically. The house, like many during those economically trying times, was a crowded one. She was living with her grandmother, two aunts—one married and the other unmarried—and several cousins. And, of course, there was her own mother.

"Our whole family was a little unstable," she recalls. And for that reason she could not remember herself as a very funny kid during those trying years.

Her grandmother's house was located in what was then called the Haymarket District of Dayton, what would today be called a depressed area. The sight of winos sleeping it off in the street was no surprise to the people who lived there, including Erma Fiste.

"We were poor," Bombeck says. "I'd just have been *sick* if I'd known. But I thought it was a really neat neighborhood. My best friend lived over the funeral parlor and for entertainment we went to the synagogue on Saturdays and the Catholic church on Sundays—and I was a *Protestant.*"

When Erma Fiste was eleven, her mother married a man named Albert Harris, whom she had met at General Motors. Harris, always called "Tom" for some unaccountable reason, became Bombeck's stepfather, and the three of them moved away from grandmother's. Although they were not at all affluent, the pressure on the growing girl abated.

She was just reaching her teens. She was not the most popular girl in class, nor was she the least popular. She was somewhere plunk in the middle. However, she began to show an extraordinary interest in reading. It was something to do, and it whetted her appetite for the big world out there.

Her favorite reading became humor, and not "kid" humor comics, but the real thing.

"When everybody else was reading Nancy Drew mysteries," Bombeck explains, "I was reading Robert Benchley, James Thurber, and H. Allen Smith. Their books were high on my Christmas list."

She would send her mother into a department store with the names of books she wanted to read. Mrs. Fiste (Harris) would read off the titles to the clerk, and would shrug apologetically at the incredulous expression on the back of the book salesman.

"She wants this. I don't know why. The kid's a little strange." At least, that was the way Bombeck remembers it. "She felt she had to apologize," she said about her mother. Nevertheless, her mother, one of the "gutsiest" ladies Bombeck knows, made sure that her daughter had the books she wanted, and, later on, had the college education she wanted.

The humor books cast a spell over Bombeck. "From about the seventh grade on," she says, "I know exactly what I wanted to do. I wanted to write and I wanted to write humor."

In fact, she began writing one year later in the eighth grade: "I wrote funny poetry."

There was something about her roots—Dayton, Ohio—that seemed to stimulate her interest in humor.

"Ohio spawns funny people," she says today. "Take Tim Conway, James Thurber, Paul Lynde, Jonathan Winters, Phyllis Diller—the list of funny folks from Ohio goes right up your arm."

In fact, she feels there might be a good reason for it. "The only thing I can figure is that when you consider the presidents who came from Ohio, you could just laugh for about fifty years."

Who were they? Read the list and . . . weep!

Ulysses S. Grant. Rutherford B. Hayes. James A. Garfield. Benjamin Harrison. William McKinley. William Howard Taft. Warren G. Harding.

"When I was fourteen, Dorothy Thompson, the news correspondent, came to town for a lecture." Even if Dorothy Thompson wasn't a humorist, she was a successful writer, and Bombeck wasn't going to pass up an opportunity to see a genuine correspondent.

"I was coming down with measles, but I was absolutely ruthless in my need to see her." And so Erma Fiste went, regardless of her condition or her degree of contagion. "I infected the entire hall that night!"

Later that year, she begged her mother to buy her a Dorothy Thompson book for her Christmas present. It cost five dollars—a lot of money in those days. That book put a big hole in the Christmas budget. "Mother, God bless her, bought it," Bombeck says, "even though she thought writing was simple-minded."

Making It in Journalism

At Patterson Vocational High School in Dayton, the school program required students to alternate their classes with work experience. Erma Fiste landed a job as copy girl and part-time secretary at Dayton's morning paper, the *Herald*, which is now the *Journal-Herald*.

She would work two weeks in class, and then two weeks at the newspaper. At school she wrote a humor column for the school paper. There were people there who were trying to help anyone who had a little talent. "A high school English teacher, Jim Harris, encouraged me tremendously," Bombeck recalls. "He dogged me about my education."

At the newspaper she typed letters, took dictation, and also wrote stories. Her first break came when the feature editor thought it might be cute to have her interview Shirley Temple.

"I did it from the angle that we were both sixteen and probably had lots in common," Bombeck says. "We didn't."

The story, even though it was about the famous child star of the Thirties, didn't even make the front page. Nor did another story she wrote later on which she thought was a natural.

"I had one all set to go. I was so excited. Then somebody crossed the Rhine, some army or something."

It was at Patterson Vocational that Erma Fiste met William Lawrence Bombeck, the man who was later to become her husband. Both of them were taking classes under the same school program, studying and working, and both were interested in journalism. Erma worked on the morning paper, the *Herald*; Bill worked as copy boy on the afternoon paper, the *Journal*.

"We had the most exciting job around. He was covering high school sports and I was on features, radio listings, and obituaries."

She graduated from high school in 1944. Luckily, she was able to convert her earlier part-time job at the newspaper into a full-time job as a copy girl, and stayed there for a year.

It was at the *Dayton Herald* that Erma Fiste met Phillis Battelle, who later went on to become a syndicated newspaper columnist. Battelle remembered Erma Fiste vividly and wrote about her in a magazine article.

Batelle was "the lowly reporter writing obituaries," and Erma Fiste was "even lowlier—the copy girl," Battelle recalled. She remembered Erma as "a bouncy kid in bobby socks, knife-pleated skirts, and baggy sweaters."

The columnist knew Erma Fiste was made of superior stuff. "She was destined to go places even back then—usually to the arcade around the corner, to buy coffee and sweet rolls for editors.

"We didn't realize at the time that under the tawny curls there resided the whacko psyche of a young genius who could find humor in everything. Especially in life's tragedies and drudgeries."

By then Bill Bombeck was eligible for the draft. World War II, which was actually winding down, was still raging in 1944, and Bombeck signed up for the army. He left his job for the service in 1945.

That same year Erma Fiste quite her job as copy girl and applied for admission to the University of Ohio. She had saved up a bit of money for her education, and her mother and stepfather were willing to help as much as they could. She was accepted in 1945, and began her studies that fall. She studied one year at Ohio and then transferred to the University of Dayton for the following three.

Majoring in English, she devised a schedule that involved only morning classes so she could work in the afternoons and on weekends. It was a tough go, but it was fruitful. She was able to write a humor column for the student newspaper and magazine. Her outside jobs were many and varied.

She did public relations work for the local YMCA, and edited a shoppers' newspaper. In addition to that, she also wrote a column for a department store house organ, and handled—wouldn't you know it?—a termite-control account for an advertising agency.

It was during her college years that Erma Fiste decided to change her religious affiliation from Protestant to Roman Catholic.

The war was soon over for Bill Bombeck, and when he returned to Dayton, he enrolled at the University of Dayton and tried to make up for lost time. He was then one full year behind Erma.

After four years of working in the afternoons and studying at night, Erma Fiste graduated from the university with a B.A. degree in English.

Not long thereafter, on August 13, 1949, she and Bill Bombeck were married. Erma then was able to get a full-time job on the *Dayton Herald*, while her husband, making up for the education time he had lost, continued at the university. He graduated with an A.B. in education in 1950, and soon got a job teaching at nearby Centerville High School.

"I was teaching everything back then: spelling, science, English, history, sociology, government, and arithmetic," he recalls.

The newly married Bombecks moved to Centerville to sample the suburban life.

Meanwhile, Erma was again working at the *Journal-Herald*, writing obituaries at first but finally winding up in the women's department.

She was now a full-fledged reporter, and able to fly with the best of them. But she was, in her own opinion, a cut below most of her peers. As a reporter, she was, in her words, "Bad! Extremely bad."

"I remember once," she recalls, "I went with a group of teenagers on a study tour to Washington and New York. I accompanied the kids. This was the first year they opened up the Russian embassy and we got to go through it. And my editor wrote me and said, 'You covered that like a tea party.' He was right—my story was ridiculous."

As for the stories she covered, most of them turned out to be society pieces, women's features and those ubiquitous obituaries.

"I never took a note so whoever I interviewed—even Eleanor Roosevelt—came out sounding just like me."

"Every once in a while," she recalls, "I tried to inject a humorous personal story—about some domestic thing such as going on a vacation—but newspapers were not very receptive to humor in the 1940s. Occasionally a humorous story would run."

She eventually wound up writing a women's page column that was, in her words, "a sort of sick Heloise. . . . I told people to go clean their johns, lock them up, and send the kids to the gas station at the corner." The column was called "Operation Dustrag," in which she "took on housework, if you can make housework humorous." Apparently she did so. However, most of the readers, in those pre–Equal Rights Amendment days, didn't really appreciate it.

"In the 1940s, you didn't make fun of domestic chores. Housework was a religious experience!"

In 1953, the Bombecks' first child, a daughter named Betsy, was born. Erma Bombeck quit work and settled down in the home to bring up the children.

"Andy came along in 1955," she says, "followed by Matthew.

"I didn't do anything except blow up sterilizers for ten or eleven years." Of course, she did succeed, as she put it, in putting on weight and overbleaching her clothes, and watching her yellow-wax buildup.

But for Erma Bombeck, those in-between years were much more than simply marking time and waiting for the inevitable moment when she would be faced with the empty nest and would be able to fly, full-fledged, back into journalism.

While she lived in the suburbs, she tried hard to be a good homemaker. "I really worked on it for a very long time," she says. Later on her daughter once asked her how she was able to *stand* it. Her reply: "I worked hard at it."

"I would take decorating classes," Bombeck recalls. "I would crochet little knobs for the doorknobs with Santa Claus and whiskers. I'd make taffy for the kids, take them on field trips. Volunteered like crazy. I just kept very busy."

All in all, "It was a lot of fun," she once said. "I even enjoyed scrubbing an occasional floor."

Bombeck Tries Her Last Shot

Even though she had traded in being a full-fledged reporter for being a full-fledged housewife, Erma Bombeck still nourished her dream of being a full-fledged humor writer during her years of bearing and rearing children.

"You have to dream to write humor," she once told a well-wisher. "It is a matter of looking at tragedy and dreaming up some humor in it. That way, you survive. If you don't take yourself seriously, it's sure as heck you're not going to take anything else seriously.

"I always had a philosophy, even when the kids were little. They'd be bleeding, and I'd take them to the emergency ward and say, 'Doctor, can this be fixed?' and as long as it could, I'd say, 'Okay, kids, it's no big deal.' That's the kind of person I am. Manic, very manic.''

In 1963 her last child, Matthew, entered kindergarten. Now, finally, Bombeck had a chance to take a deep breath and look around her during those loose hours of the morning. And not only did she see what was around her for the first time in a number of years, but she also saw herself and what she had become.

"You get so you think you can't do anything but get stains out of bibs," she says.

"I was looking at the ads in the magazines that say 'Earn money—address envelopes at one cent apiece,' and wondering. Could I do that? Could I? It's a terrible transition from a housewife, but you just have to do something that isn't routine. Join a club, get a job—you just gotta have something else."

She knew she had to do *something*, but what?

"I was thirty-seven—too old for a paper route, too young for social security, and too tired for an affair.

"I was like every other woman whose children are growing," she recalls, "wondering whether or not to take the plunge and go back to work. It's awful. You lie to yourself. You say, 'I could write *the book* this year, but I have to paint the kitchen, and I don't want any distractions once I start *the book.*' The truth is, you're scared you might fall on your face and that would be your last shot, lady."

Ironically enough, it was at just about this time in her life that a man moved in across the street from her Centerville home who was a local television news reporter just getting started.

His name was Phil Donahue.

She first saw him wandering around on his new front lawn, trying to dislodge a diaper from his new toilet. The memorable words of their first meeting are unfortunately lost to history. But she did welcome him to the joys of suburbia.

If this were fiction, Bombeck would think: "Donahue can do it. Why can't I?"

No such thing occurred. But Bombeck was working out something in her mind and eventually she psyched herself up for the big try. Actually, it was not all that *big* a try, but it was a try. What she knew the most about was being a housewife and mother. And that was what she wanted to tell others.

"I found much of it funny, and human, so I decided to write about it."

She put together a few column ideas and took them in to Ron Ginger, the editor of the *Kettering-Oakwood Times*. The *K-O Times* was a weekly newspaper with a circulation of about 12,000. Ginger decided to let her take a shot at a regular feature.

"I began with a column called 'Zone 57'—that was our post office code in Centerville, Ohio—for the Kettering-Oakwood weekly newspaper, which covered our Dayton suburbs. I got three dollars a column, and it ran once a week."

It was what she called a humor column on the "utility-room beat." She wrote the column for about a year and a half.

Actually, it was against Ginger's better judgment that he hired her for the column. However, the reaction to "Zone 57" was so positive that the newspaper entered it in a state newswriting competition not once, but twice.

It didn't even get honorable mention.

However, there was a lot of demand from women's groups for Erma Bombeck as a guest speaker. She began to make personal appearances at a modest fee.

The newspaper, realizing that she *was* popular, assigned her to cover a regular story for them. It was a football game.

Donald Wright, now editor of the *K-O Times*, recalls: "She wrote a hilarious piece about the people in the stands, and handled the game itself in the final sentence."

It was a great gag—and a typical Bombeck joke.

But for the hard-nosed editors, it was the end of her straight reporting career.

Two nonmentions in a statewide competition and a real fumble at regular reporting—to mix the metaphor, three strikes and you're out? No way.

Just about that time, like a budding actress who is discovered by a talent scout, she was "discovered," as she put it, "by a reader."

He was Glenn Thompson, executive editor of the *Dayton Journal-Herald*. He had read one of her columns in the *K-O Times*.

"I didn't know him," she says. "We had never met, but if there is one person in this world who is responsible for what I have done, it's that man. I got a letter from him saying he'd like me to write a regular humor column for his editorial page. Without further ado, he signed me up to do three columns a week."

She got a big raise—$15 apiece for each column, or $12 more per column than she had got from the *K-O Times*. That was a 400 percent raise. With that kind of escalation, who knew where it would end?

"Ginger was a friend of mine," Thompson says, "so I had warned him that I was going to steal his columnist. He was pleased that Erma would be doing better. It didn't take me long to satisfy myself that Erma could be funny three times a week."

Dayton's readers liked Bombeck's column as well as Thompson did. Within three weeks Thompson had put together a batch of her columns and sent them to Tom Dorsey at Newsday Syndicate on Long Island, New York. Dorsey liked the Bombeck touch too.

"Tom came to Dayton and had dinner with Erma and me," Thompson says. He told Dorsey that she was in tune with suburbanite women all over the country.

"You've got to give her a bigger audience," he pleaded.

Dorsey agreed. Newsday Syndicate took her on in 1965 with a thrice-weekly column titled "At Wit's End," as one of the Newsday Specials.

"I did nothing," Bombeck recalls. "I just watched it all happen."

"I was paying $45 a week for Erma," Thompson recalls, sounding very much like Erma Bombeck. "When the syndicate took her over I was able to buy her for $15!"

Into the Big Time

The column grew at a fairly respectable rate, with the syndicate adding on a newspaper here and there, and the column gaining readership at an increasing, but not really devastating, rate.

In 1967 the Los Angeles Times Syndicate took over the Newsday Syndicate. The Bombeck column was being used by sixty-five newspapers. Her contract was on a year-to-year basis.

On the strength of the column's success, she interested *Good Housekeeping* magazine in a monthly column, "Up the Wall." In addition to that regular column, which appeared from 1969 to 1974, she contributed numerous freelance pieces to *Reader's Digest, Family Circle, Redbook,* and *McCall's.*

During the first five years of the newspaper column's existence, 1965 to 70, Bombeck went on the lecture circuit not only to earn extra money but also to help push her column. But she kept her lectures to a maximum of six or eight appearances yearly.

"I can't be gone more than two days because that's all the underwear we have," she told Betty Dunn in a story about her for *Life* magazine in 1971.

"I don't know why women come to hear me, yet I used to do the same thing," Bombeck recalls. "Go to endless trouble, get a babysitter, park the car. I used to buy a season ticket to the Dayton Town Hall lectures and sit there listening to Vance Packard."

A Change in the Lifestyle

It was during a lecture tour in 1969 that she spoke in Phoenix. "I got on the plane in Chicago, in a blizzard, and I got off in Phoenix at midnight, with a warm breeze slapping at me. I asked myself then, 'What am I doing back there in Dayton?' "

When she returned home, she discussed the situation with her husband and the family.

Bill Bombeck was doing very well in Dayton, rising in the public school system, first as a principal and then as a supervisor of social studies in the Dayton school system. By that time, Betsy was eighteen, a freshman at the University of Colorado; Andy was sixteen, and Matt was thirteen.

The Bombecks had just purchased a thirty-acre farm in Bellbrook, Ohio, on the outskirts of Dayton. "We finally got the farm we'd always wanted," Bombeck recalls. "The horses for the kids, the rolling grounds, the trails. Then we discovered that was not what we really wanted. The house was really something, but we just couldn't keep up with it."

When Erma Bombeck made the big suggestion to the family—that is, to move to Phoenix—everyone sat around and stared at one another. No one really knew whether or not to make such a big change.

For one, Bill Bombeck didn't like the idea at all. He had no desire to be a will-o'-the-wisp attached to his wife's apronstrings. What about his career?

"I finally won him over by pointing out that the last three school levies had failed, and that if we moved he could take time off and complete work on his doctorate,'' Bombeck says. Then, with typical Bombeck aplomb: "Also, he owed me a honeymoon which we could take."

He finally did buy the idea, but it was hard work selling him.

"We didn't take a vote," Bombeck says. "If you think we are a democratic family, you're crazy."

The change was not an easy thing for her readers to assimilate.

"When we left to go west, people said, oh, you're leaving the grass roots," she remembers. "Everybody thinks *they* live in the grass roots. They think that in Arizona, in Ohio. The most flattering thing to me is that people think I live in the town where they read me.

"Once I wrote I was so bored I couldn't stand it all: all there was to do was sit around and watch the garden hose swell. It was winter and our hose in Ohio was frozen—we'd been too lazy to bring it in. In Arizona I learned that they thought it was swelling from the heat."

Bombeck notes: "Every winter I cope with snow shovels and other problems of the season. I do them from memory. Who can be a typical mother in a climate like Arizona's?"

The move didn't change the Bombeck lifestyle much. The kids were growing up and going out of the house one by one. The new place was a $100,000 home in the shadow of Camelback Mountain. "We look right into his nostrils," she says of the camel.

There was a swimming pool in the back, surrounded by Dwarf Tiff grass watered periodically by sprinklers automated and computerized to turn on and off at the proper, healthful intervals.

Once in Phoenix, Bill Bombeck enrolled at Arizona State University at Tempe, and began working on his doctorate in education.

Bombeck was amused at the situation that developed when she applied for personal credit in Phoenix.

"What does your husband do?" she was asked.

"He goes to school."

"What do you do?"

"I work for a syndicate."

She got her credit anyway.

When her husband earned his doctorate in education, he then resumed his career, as an educator-administrator in the Phoenix school system.

By 1975 he was house director of the division of Trevor Brown High School in Phoenix, one of the largest secondary schools in the city. Later he became its principal.

The children enrolled in school and continued on their way. In her newfound and now flourishing career, Bombeck was writing about her own life—as any author does. However, she made it a point never to write specifically about any one of her children.

She felt their privacy was worth too much to sacrifice.

As for her husband Bill—the "husband" in her columns is Bill and it isn't Bill. It's a composite of all husbands and of her husband.

"Being a character in Erma's columns has been no problem," Bill says. "She's been writing humor about the things around her as long as I can remember, and anyone around Erma must expect to be part of her funny world."

To update the family to the present day:

The oldest child, Betsy, is now a computer saleswoman in her late twenties.

Andy, the middle one, is now a schoolteacher, in his twenties.

Matt, the youngest, aspires to be a film-maker and is currently between engagements—or, more precisely, in front of engagements.

You'll never read about any of them as themselves in the Bombeck column, however. Each has his own privacy and individualism.

To update Bill Bombeck: at present he has given up his

job in the world of education to take over the immense and sprawling empire of Erma Bombeck's income. That's right: he's her financial manager.

Life with Mother

In 1974 Bombeck's "stage mother" reached retirement age, and both she and her husband—the one unaccountably called Tom but named Albert—pulled up stakes at General Motors and moved down from Dayton to Arizona. Their target was Sun City, a suburb of Phoenix—and about twenty-three miles away from the Bombeck household.

"We don't want to live in their back yard," says Erma Harris. "And we just love Sun City. Everybody's retired here and they've got time for you. All our neighbors are like our Sun City family."

Erma Harris worked on the production line at GM for many years; Tom was in the safety division.

She admits that they do get a lot of attention from their neighbors because of her relationship to her very visible and successful daughter.

"Of course we're proud of her."

She admits that most of the things written about her in the column are true—"but when she said I have permacrinkles and varicose veins—why, I don't even *have* varicose veins." Then she laughs, in a typically Bombeck fashion. "But I started *looking* for them."

The Harrises usually watch their daughter on television. "We always take a nap in the afternoon so we can stay awake when she's going to be on the Johnny Carson show. It's so late."

Once Erma Harris was on the phone talking to her daughter, and she suddenly realized what time it was. "Oh, I've got to hang up because Erma's on!"

And on the other end of the line, she heard her daughter's protesting voice: "Mother—."

Bombeck's Dog-Eared Children

As her own children began to grow up and leave the house, Bombeck began producing still another kind of offspring in addition to her newspaper columns—books.

The first, as noted, was a compilation of her columns, also titled *At Wit's End*. The book sold briskly, but it was no blockbuster. To give her more clout, Doubleday teamed her up with Bil Keane, a cartoonist whose main interest—the suburban family—was the same as Bombeck's, but from a masculine viewpoint. Their first collaborated book was titled *Just Wait Till You Have Children of Your Own*. Published in 1971, it did fairly well.

Her third book, *I Lost Everything in the Postnatal Depression*, was published by Doubleday in 1973.

Thus by the middle 1970s, Erma Bombeck not only was a firmly established commodity on the women's pages of suburban newspapers, but was also beginning to be recognized as the author of books. And her frequent appearances on television to push her product in turn spawned another facet of her success.

She was signed up to appear twice a week on ABC-TV's new show "Good Morning, America." These vignettes consisted of 190-second segments—some of them pure soliloquies, and others of them interviews with interesting people, animals, or other oddities.

It was partially because of the television appearances and partially because of the continual snowballing of her name that Erma Bombeck's fourth book, *The Grass Is Always Greener over the Septic Tank*, became a genuine bestseller. It remained on the lists for nearly a year and sold the astonishing number of over a half-million hardcover copies alone.

The book even became a made-for-television motion picture, which starred Carol Burnett and Charles Grodin and which appeared on CBS October 25, 1978. It was not a critical success.

Her fifth book was *If Life Is a Bowl of Cherries—What Am I Doing in the Pits?* and was published in spring 1978 by McGraw-Hill. It hit the bestseller lists shortly after publication and remained there throughout the year.

Her sixth book was published in 1980 by McGraw-Hill—*Aunt Erma's Cope Book*. The book satirizes the glut of "How to Survive" tomes and advises men and women on how to cope with every situation from leaky plumbing to hot flashes. It too became an almost immediate bestseller.

Within weeks of its publication, a Broadway producer named Larry Kasha had bought the dramatic rights, and planned to produce it in conjunction with David Landay. Susan Silver, a scriptwriter, was hired from the "Mary Tyler Moore Show" to get a script in order. And Bea Arthur, star of the long-running television series "Maude," was said to be considering starring in the show.

The structure of the play was "very free form," Kasha said in an interview with Carol Lawson of the *New York Times*. "A series of vignettes. Erma talks to the audience, as George Burns did in the old 'Burns and Allen' TV shows. Susan Silver has created a story line to link the vignettes together. There are sequences about people jogging, going through therapy—whatever the latest fad is."

As if all that wasn't enough, Bombeck herself decided to delve once again into the deep and oftentimes fatal waters of prime-time television. After all, she had made a breakthrough in morning television; why not the big time?

Early in 1981 she wrote and produced a pilot for a situation comedy aimed at prime-time television. Called "Maggie," the comedy is really about Bombeck herself and the "family" she writes about. Maggie is a married woman with three kids who does all the things women with kids do these days in the suburbs of America.

The show was videotaped in Phoenix and shipped off to New York where the network heads at ABC-TV started to ponder it. Apparently the pilot was considered strong enough for inclusion on the fall schedule of the network, for sure enough, the May 9-15, 1981, issue of *TV Guide* contained notification of the show as an already sketched-in prime-time entry.

Slated to appear on Fridays at 9 on ABC-TV, it is categorized as a "comedy about family life in suburbia."

Bombeck apparently had some reservations about the project—at least in public. "During the taping," she told Maggie Wilson of the *Phoenix Republic*, "I got so tired of hearing the same lines again and again I was ready to throw up. So if they say no, I don't think I'll weep."

However: "If they say yes, I'll work myself into a happy froth and carry on."

They said yes. And so Bombeck began revving up for a grueling season of extra work. Bill Bombeck sighed and bought a bigger ledger to keep track of the Bombeck income.

Bombeck's current earnings are not known, but in 1978, she was estimated to be earning at least a half-million dollars a year. And she sold paperback rights to one book for a million. Not bad for a housewife with nothing more to her credit than a sense of humor.

Bombeck's humor is deliberate, not accidental. She works hard at getting laughs. She never does place a foot or word wrong without studied intent.

How does she manage it? Who are her models? How does she get her ideas? And where is she going from here?

Chapter 2

Bombeckiana—I

Three Times a Week—Plus

Although it was the publication of her books that made Erma Bombeck a respectable humorist and got her name mentioned in all the newspapers and magazines as a top, bestselling humor writer, it was and is still her syndicated newspaper column that forms the main body of her work.

Her early books were simply reissues of her columns, albeit with a bit of transitional work to tie them together. We'll look at the books later on. Her twice-a-week stint on the "Good Morning, America" show for ABC-TV is a kind of adaptation of her column humor to the visual medium. We'll see how she does it in another section.

The newspaper column has always been an interesting phenomenon in the American press. There are good columnists and poor ones. Right now the average newspaper runs perhaps a dozen or so columns each day—on politics, on science, on household problems, on romance, on astrological forecasts, on finance.

And on humor.

The production of a column has its advantages and its drawbacks, chief of which is the constant pressure to "get out a column" even though the columnist may have no idea in the head. But usually the idea does come.

And the advantages outweigh the disadvantages. Because there is a strict rhythm to the appearance of the column, a blockbuster of an idea is not demanded every day. The pacing can vary. One day a lightweight idea will do; another day a very serious idea will work. There is always endless variety.

Because of the restrictions of space, the column must be written to the same length each day so the layout specialists can figure out exactly how much room to allot to the day's offering. Bombeck's basic length is somewhere between 350 and 400 words, with the average falling at 375. That's about two typed pages, double-spaced, depending on the width of the margins.

The stricture of space is both a good and a bad thing. Sometimes it is a problem to find the 375 words. Other times the problem is to cut down a good idea so it will fit into the space. It takes much work—drive, determination, sweat, and talent—to bring it off.

Some fancy columnists equate writing a column to working within the strictures of the sonnet, either Petrarchan or Shakespearean. It isn't exactly that, although the format certainly creates a kind of prepackaged product.

There is a matter of timeliness in column writing. The humorist especially must keep up to date on all the things that are happening everywhere—things around the home, things on television, things in books, things in magazines, things in the newspapers. She must know who the main political personalities are, the star show-business talents, the movers and shakers of the world, and even the names of the grubby little people in rock groups.

The more typical Erma Bombeck is, the less typically she writes. Let's take a look at how she works it all out in some samples of her thrice-weekly column.

Number One on a Scale of One to Ten

Self-depreciation is the most important tool in the humorist's bag of tricks. It is no accident that Rodney Dangerfield has made it his entire comic shtick: "I get no respect!" Bombeck uses it constantly when she pictures herself as the trying-to-cope-but-barely-succeeding housewife, the slightly overweight, slightly exhausted, slightly ineffectual woman of the house, overwhelmed by appliances, budgets, and kids.

The Bombeck that is the put-upon housewife is hardly the world's idea of the most beautiful woman in the world—the Number Ten, in the current jargon, on a scale of one to ten—hardly, in short, the sex symbol of the free world.

Bombeck flirts with the idea of being a gorgeous Number Ten, and decides that she would probably be judged Number One. Of course, she feels that she should only score herself after getting herself ready for the contest. And that means psyching herself up for the fray.

"I've had my 'goal in life' for almost a year now," she writes. "Got it last August. Up until that time I referred to it as a 'fantasy,' but somewhere along the line 'fantasy' became an *out* word and 'goal' took its place."

She explains what her goal is: "to get body in shape, raise my consciousness level, go to Hollywood, become a sex symbol, work for world peace, and 'feel good about myself.' "

These two paragraphs seem simple but are exceedingly complex, and are typical Bombeck. In those two paragraphs she does several things simultaneously that set the theme and draw a bead on the subject she will satirize.

First, she selects a type of article that is familiar to all newspaper readers, the self-help piece that regularly appears in print: how to keep the body fit; how to keep the psyche in shape; how to help others; how to achieve psychological calm.

She then lumps various types of self-help articles together, with the peculiar buzz words that each type employs, and parodies them.

For example:

"Getting the body in shape" is a cliché used constantly in articles on health and beauty in magazines.

"Raising the consciousness level" is another bromide that is familiar to all readers of pieces on group therapy; it is catchy enough to be recognized, but actually means very little. Again, it is hip jargon rather than a phrase with true meaning.

"Becoming a sex symbol" is the alleged dream of every young girl. It is even more the alleged dream of every middle-aged woman. In point of fact, it is exactly what Bombeck calls it—a "fantasy." But she pretends it isn't.

"Working for world peace" is one of those lofty goals everyone reads about in the popular magazines. Unselfish dedication is a good antidote for the selfish "me-first" attitude of the current generation; indulging in such a vague enterprise is also a relief from the hard work of the job or of the house.

"Feeling good about oneself" is another cliché similar to "raising the consciousness level." It too enjoys current popularity in the mass circulation journals. Like its counterpart, it means absolutely nothing in itself, but *sounds* interesting. This dreary bromide is heard almost every night on television talk shows, from the lips of actresses and career women, particularly those who have suddenly had fame and fortune thrust upon them and must prove that their lives are not really "empty" and "unfulfilled." If one is rich and famous, it is almost obligatory to "feel good about oneself."

By jumbling these phrases in the same sentence, and letting them battle one another, Bombeck creates a short catalogue of the basically meaningless jargon used in self-help writing.

But that is all technique. What she is really satirizing is the whole point of the "goal in life" bit that the typical self-help article sets up for the reader. Usually the reader's "goal in life" will be a return to the job market, the thing many mothers and housewives are wistfully thinking about as they raise their children.

Bombeck skews the term to include psyching oneself up to meeting the challenges of society and putting oneself in competition against others to win fame and fortune.

But at the same time she carefully lays a time-bomb in the lead paragraph which is bound to blow up before the piece is through. "Goal in life," she says, once meant "fantasy." Obviously, it still does. She just pretends it doesn't.

Like most humorists, Bombeck is skilled at twisting clichés into catch phrases. An "in-word" is a word that is currently in usage; there is no such term as "out-word"; but, logically, there should be. Bombeck uses it.

To realize her "goal in life," Bombeck looks around for a "role model" to imitate. Again, the phrase "role model" is familiar sociological jargon. She sees in the television schedules that Barbara Walters is going to interview Bo Derek, Farrah Fawcett, Cheryl Ladd, and Bette Midler.

"Merciful heavens!" she continues. Here are four role models to pattern her life upon!

But the superstars are so overpowering in their beauty and charisma that Bombeck feels she cuts a completely ridiculous figure in comparison to any one of them. She watches enviously as they are interviewed by Walters.

"They are all sex symbols, all had great bodies, knew who they were and were in touch with their feelings. They were mobbed by fans wherever they went, had big houses with fresh flowers on every table, faces pretty enough to offset stringy hair, and men who masterminded their every move."

Again, typical Bombeck. In describing the four role

models, she uses elements from self-help articles to depict their unattainability. "They knew who they were": a phrase the opposite of "searching for their identity," a cliché of the self-help articles. "They were in touch with their feelings": again, lifted right out of self-help jargon, the opposite of those poor creatures in dire stress who have "lost touch" with their feelings.

Note the juxtaposition of exaggeration and understatement in the next sentence as Bombeck shuffles the reality of the commonplace with the fantasy of the superstate: "mobbed by fans" (superstatus), "big houses" (superstatus), "with fresh flowers on every table" (superstatus, but strictly housewifey in point of view), "faces pretty enough to offset stringy hair" (commonplace mixed with superstatus), and "men who masterminded their every move" (fantasy from the dreaming housewife). It's the mix that produces her humor.

"All four," she goes on, "were at the peak of success and in the state of 'mis.' Misquoted, misguided, misled, misunderstood, mismatched, mismanaged, mismated, misinterpreted and misrepresented. And miserable.

"Yes, on a scale of one to ten, not one of them came in under a nine. The only thing I can figure out is that I have been calculating the 'ten' phenomenon on the wrong scale. These women are obviously grading on the 'curve.' If they say they're a 'ten' at the beach, it must depend on how much sand they're buried in, how much water they're retaining, and how many threes and fours are around."

Bombeck peels the varnish off the truth for the reader. In reality, the subjects are all "miserable." In the myth, all call themselves "nine on a scale of ten." Note the nifty intrusion of the middle-suburbia school yard phrase "grading on the 'curve,' " to underline the difference. And then comes Bombeck's fantasy-turned-upside-down—"how much sand they're buried in, how much water they're retaining, and how many threes and fours are around."

The myth that Bombeck starts out to explore is now a peeled-down onion of reality. The coach has turned back into a pumpkin; the steeds are mice.

"All I know is out of four sex symbols interviewed, one had a child, one had a husband, one had an understanding mother, and one had peace of mind."

And then her devastating punch line:

"I have all four. That makes me a 'twenty' and still looking for a role model who deserves me."

The point of the piece is obvious. The fantasy of superstatus is easily shot down. The realities that the superstars seek—a child, a husband, an understanding mother, peace of mind—are exactly what Bombeck, and the most commonplace of all of us, already have.

Note that even though the piece starts out as a satire on self-help articles, the main thrust of the argument, and the real point, is something else again. Here, as in many cases, the parody becomes a medium to allow the humorist to attack a completely unrelated object.

How to Make It to the Pits Without Hardly Trying

Not all of any humorist's works have that much of a moral to them. Many of Bombeck's are simply extensions of one very simple idea either carried to an absurdity, or expanded with off-the-top-of-the-head examples or laundry lists of laughs.

The business of oneupmanship occurs in many different forms, some of them peculiar to the middle-class members of suburbia. Travel, which at one time was the province only of the very rich, is now the principal recreation of the moderately affluent. In suburbia the ideal is to be the first on your block to visit, oh, say, Minsk or Pinsk. However, with the big jets going almost everywhere these days, the name place becomes not the target for the pacesetter, but some isolated esoteric site in the name place.

And there's the added fillip of taking countless pictures of the places visited and showing them to friends back home. Once it was fun. But now, when *everyone* has cameras, photographing all corners of the earth . . .

"Every time my husband and I take a trip, we have visions of coming home and sharing it with our friends," Bombeck writes. "We don't expect to enter the city on donkeys traveling streets lined with palm-carrying enthusiasts, or deliver a message from a hillside while thousands sit at rapt attention.

"But is it too much to ask for a small group to listen politely and occasionally say, 'That sounds wonderful,' or 'I hope you took pictures'?"

Bombeck uses the time-honored tradition of exaggeration—the tall-tales syndrome—in her opening: the image of entering the city on donkeys traveling streets lined with palm-carrying enthusiasts; the picture of delivering a message from a hillside while thousands sit at rapt attention. A little honest exaggeration, particularly with a biblical touch, never hurts.

After the opening, the theme—oneupmanship—is developed quickly.

Bombeck tells about returning from a trip to Greece and telling guests about seeing the Acropolis by day and night, Hadrian's Arch, Mt. Lycabettus, Constitution Square, the Royal Gardens, the Stadium, the Athens Cathedral, the National Archaeological Museum, the Gennadeion, Daphni, Eleusis, Piraeus, the Temple of Poseidon and Cape Sounion.

Which would seem to be a fairly full itinerary. But wait. . . .

The putdown comes almost immediately. "You didn't eat at Styros Herculonburger?" one guest cries out in dismay. "Then you didn't see Greece!"

Nasty? Of course. Although Bombeck is warm and decent, she sees suburbia with the X-ray eyes of a realist. She sees and hears the contempt and the envy. They puncture her ego.

But that's only a beginning.

The putdown artist does not work alone. All the way to Greece, he cries to his wife, and the Bombecks didn't even have a Herculonburger!

No Herculonburger? Mrs. Putdown wails back. Then maybe the Bombecks didn't even go to see the world-famous Athos Flea Market!

Naturally the Bombecks are overpowered by the twin thrusts of the double-pronged attack. When Bombeck asks where the Athos Flea Market is, there's no answer. Instead, the Putdowns launch another attack:

Probably, they suggest, the Bombecks even got taken buying fake curios—like 500-year-old icons! (Of course they did!)

And at the bottom of the pit wallows Bombeck, the Little Woman.

The point of the skit is made. But this leaves room for a little elaboration, and the elaboration becomes a series of one-liners, as Bombeck herself tops each putdown with another. These elaborations may be pure fantasy, sprinkled with a bit of sarcasm.

Bombeck introduces the one-liners by saying that the trip to Greece isn't any exception; every time the Bombecks go away anywhere, well-traveled "friends" put them down.

For example, when they went to Rome and saw the pope, the putdown was: "You didn't meet his boss?"

What can top that line? Not much, actually. But there is more.

When they went to Hawaii, the reaction was: "You missed Don Ho?"

When they went to Florida: "Too bad! You missed the alligators!"

End of column? No way.

The main joke of the skit is complete, along with a laundry list of one-liners by way of elaboration, showing the reader how to continue the game.

Bombeck decides oneupmanship artists needn't always win. But how to beat them? How, when they've obviously defeated their host and hostess?

"As my husband flipped the switch on the projector to show the first of 700 slides," Bombeck writes, "I turned off the lights and locked the door. 'You missed your chance,' I smiled."

Punch line and fade out.

In this case, the payoff is simply a twist to put at the end of the column to end it, a kind of O. Henry ending to the extended anecdote.

The basic joke illustrating the oneupmanship theme is what Stan and Doris do to the Bombecks. The payoff line—the oneupper being oneupped from an entirely different direction—is simply to return things to the status quo.

There are deficiencies in the Bombeck humor, some of which are revealed in the oneupmanship piece. Although the "Styros Herculonburger" is a funny enough name for a restaurant—a kind of sideways takeoff on an imagined Styros's Hercules-sized Hamburger Joint—Bombeck's mentor, Robert Benchley, had a bit more success in making up wacky fake names of places. In one piece he mentioned spending a summer in the "medieval Spanish province Las Los (or Los Las, as it was formerly called, either way meaning 'The The,' pl.)."

Come and Get It—Wherever You Are

No one can dramatize the day-to-day frustrations and anxieties of being a housewife better than Bombeck can.

The tinier the problem, the bigger she makes it. In this she is the equal of Benchley, who had a talent for seizing upon a tiny frustration or annoyance and turning it into the subject of a whole article.

Cooking is one of a housewife's most onerous burdens; at least at times it certainly seems to be. But it is not so much the actual cooking that is aggravating, as getting the damned items all cooked at the right time: the frozen dessert, the vegetables, the roast, the rolls, and so on.

Bombeck doesn't stop there. She goes one step further, dividing the idea into bits, as it were, and focusing on one tiny element. Getting it all on the table on time and—and then what?

In handling the idea, Bombeck departs from her general policy of using herself in the first person, as an actress in the piece. In this one she features herself as a main third-person character, "Erma Bombeck." And, because this is an infinitesimal subject, she starts out as if the subject were one of the most controversial, one of the most interesting, one of the most vital in the world.

She sets up the column by describing, in a careful parody of a typical scientific paper, the discovery of the Russian psychologist Ivan P. Pavlov.

When Pavlov prepared food for a test dog, he rang a bell. The dog, smelling the food, drooled. Having once established a feeding situation through use of food and bell simultaneously, Pavlov then rang the bell *without* preparing the food; the dog immediately began to drool in spite of the fact that it could smell no food at all. A monumental scientific discovery!

Then Bombeck's parody:

"In the late 40s, Erma Bombeck, a simple housewife in Ohio, made another interesting scientific discovery. By announcing to her family, 'Dinner is ready,' it was noted that the entire family swung into action like a precision drill team."

Everyone has some sudden "chore" totally unrelated to eating: her husband rushes out to clean the medicine closet; one offspring makes a phone call; another locks herself in the bathroom; Bombeck mentions that one of them even once "took a bus to Detroit."

As the piece proceeds, the parody becomes more pronounced: Bombeck's column is a burlesque case history. The phrase "it was noted" is typical.

Soon Bombeck doesn't even bother to announce dinner. Merely the sight of her at the door causes each member of her family to vanish in one direction or another. Concerned and frustrated, Bombeck observes "yet another phenomenon."

(More scientific jargon in the form of a cliché: "She observed yet another phenomenon.")

The "phenomenon" is the telephone. As soon as everyone is seated and ready to eat, a strange thing happens. The phone always rings.

Through her parody, she has duplicated Pavlov's experiment, only in reverse. The "dog" begins to eat, and *then* the bell rings. By *not* commenting on it, Bombeck achieves a laugh and gets high points for not stepping on the joke.

The piece continues with various "experiments" as Bombeck attempts various ploys to get her family to the table on time.

She approaches them one night as they sit around the television set, and announces that she has *not* come to tell them that dinner is ready. But she doesn't fool them; they know it *is* ready. They continue to stare at the set.

She doesn't need to say they ignore their dinner; that much is obvious.

No matter what she does, as soon as the family sits down to "warm lettuce and cold french fries," individuals get up and wander off, then come back. But invariably, as soon as anyone starts eating, the phone rings.

Again, Pavlov's bell in reverse.

Bombeck determines to turn the tables. She is laid up with a virus, and her husband takes over the cooking. As he rounds up the family, "flushed with heat from the stove, and the pressure," he announces: "Dinner is ready."

The syndrome proceeds as always: one son goes to his car for his tennis racket, the dog scratches on the door to get out, another son goes out to look in the mailbox, and Erma Bombeck gets up to leave.

Her husband is beside himself. "Where are YOU going?" he asks her.

"I'm going to be sick."

"Couldn't you wait until after dinner?" he cries.

The collision of the two courses of concentration—the husband's on serving dinner, the wife's on her own nausea—is good for a laugh.

"I've worked like a dog," the husband goes on, "to get the fish sticks, the chili, and the potato chips in with the rest of the cooked food to 'come out even.' "

Later on, as the family members sit around the table, they wait for the phone to ring.

"I guess your theory has just sprung a leak," Bombeck's husband tells her. "We're eating and the phone is not ringing."

Bombeck ends: "I didn't have the heart to tell him he was only half right."

There are actually two or three currents of humor running along with each other in this piece. The use of the parody as the form in which the column is written is skillfully carried out with the phrasings and the general tone of the case history.

However, by the time the theme is set up, the parody devices mostly disappear. When the theme of housewife/cook-against-family is established, the scientific spoof is not longer needed. As Bombeck loses round after round in the battle, the self-depreciation produces several points of humor.

In the turnaround—or crisis situation—she lets her husband take over the job. Now Bombeck is working the male-female bit to its finest intensity. The take-charge husband, with the absolutely incorrigible, evasive family, loses the battle.

When he thinks he "wins," the payoff comes: Bombeck's last line—"He was only half right."

In other words, the telephone wasn't ringing; but no one was eating, either.

There's a nice incidental bit of male-female humor in the crisis situation with the husband's selection of meal ingredients: fish sticks, chili, and potato chips. What a meal! And, of course, Bombeck slips in a bit of amused irony in lumping the potato chips in with the rest of the cooked food to "come out even." An example of parenthetical humor, slipped in along the route.

Delightful in-house domestic humor.

Snatching Defeat from the Jaws of Victory

Bombeck's antagonists come at her from all directions. She gets it from her husband. She gets it from her kids. And she gets it from her own mother as well. And, of course, so does the reader, who herself is a woman who has husband, who has kids, and who has parents.

The eternal battle of the sexes takes many forms. Men do things their way; women do things theirs. Bombeck can get a whole column out of one specific manner in which the two sexes approach a problem differently.

"Hey," she writes, "I've just come up with a wonderful solution to end all wars. Let the men give directions on how to get there. Trust me. No one will be able to find it."

Bombeck claims that she has yet to follow the directions of any man to get to where she wants to go without having to ask someone else on the way the *real* directions.

The syndrome might be called direction overkill, but she prefers the term "death by instruction."

After some amusing examples, Bombeck illustrates the theme by an anecdote. A woman is lost trying to find her son's baseball team which is practicing at a place called Prindle's Field. She stops at a service station and asks the man in charge where the field is.

The man gives her elaborate instructions on how to get to Prindle's Field, explaining first where it is in relation to the expressway, and then describing an intricate series of maneuvers involving the identification of various local landmarks—with an interesting detail or two of history thrown in—and finally bringing her out at Fred's Filling Station.

The woman notices that a sign reading "Fred's Station" hangs there at the very gasoline station where she is standing. She turns to the man and, somewhat hopelessly, asks him again where Prindle's Field is.

"That's what I'm getting around to telling you," the man says. "It's behind the station."

Bombeck's comment: "Men!"

But it's not only the husband, and "men," who drive Bombeck up the wall. Her mother can do it, too.

Bombeck explains that she has always been an advocate of the pacifier, the little "rubber-plastic nipple" that can be pushed into a baby's face to keep him from crying. Bombeck confesses to keeping thirty to forty around the house in strategic spots to silence a crier in "under thirty seconds." Of course, the older generation was always adamantly opposed to such crutches.

She tells about an unexpected visit her mother pays to her house. Bombeck's daughter has a pacifier in her mouth. Her mother goes up in flames.

Bombeck pretends not to know what her mother is talking about. But her mother won't give up. She knows a pacifier when she sees one. An interrogation, with undertones of police-state menace, follows:

Where has she gotten it?

Bombeck admits that she purchased it "under the counter" at a nearby pharmacy.

Her mother begins to rant and rave. Pacifiers will make all teeth crooked, she warns; they will cause swollen lips; they will cause malocclusion of the jaw; they will cause permanent disfigurement.

Bombeck listens but won't promise not to use them in the future.

In the end, Bombeck lists the pacifier as one of the ten most significant contributions to the quality of life.

"After all," she concludes, "what other force in the world has the power to heal? To stop tears? End suffering? Sustain life? Restore world peace? And be the elixir that guarantees mothers everywhere the opportunity to sleep . . . perchance to dream?"

In the exchange, Bombeck's mother delivers herself of the usual "old wives tale" about pacifiers, and Bombeck ignores her. The touch about buying the pacifier "under the counter" puts the pacifier into the same category as birth control pills or diaphragms.

As for kids, Bombeck is always engaged in a running battle with them. One who consistently gets the best of her is the doomsayer, the modern version of the classic prophet Cassandra, who never sees anything ahead but big trouble.

Just as the family outing in the car begins, Cassandra remarks that she remembers the iron being plugged in just before they left the house. Did her mother turn it off before going out?

And so mom spends her entire vacation listening for sirens and trying to remember where she put the insurance policies.

It's Cassandra who asks her father if he really meant to leave the hose running on the lawn.

Next comes Cassandra's turn with her brother. She hints that he's keeping a stray cat hidden under his bed so he won't have to give it away.

But her brother's not the only target. Cassandra drops a hint to her sister that everyone who's been accepted at college has been notified already; where's *her* letter of acceptance?

And Cassandra has very good ears. There's a strange knock in the engine. Doesn't it sound exactly like the clanking her friend heard just before the transmission died in their car?

Now Ms. Doomsday remembers that they are headed in the same direction where she heard there were tornado warnings posted for the next three days—heard it on a newscast just before leaving the house.

They pull up to the site of the cabin the family has rented. Cassandra remembers one small detail. When her father was hiding the key under the welcome mat by the door, she noticed a man in a parked car watching from across the street.

As they walk into the cabin, Cassandra suddenly re-members that she has been exposed to measles. The rash should appear that night. If so, they can all go home the next day.

No defense against that one! The battle with kids is always a losing one.

A Smile Is a Frown Turned Upside Down

There are times when the humorist switches moods. Because she is always funny, always laughing, it seems that she has no feelings about people. But laughter, as we have seen, is quite close to tragedy; the feeling of mirth is not too different from the feeling of pain. The need to evoke laughter is sometimes the need to produce pain.

"It was one of those days when I wanted my own apartment," Bombeck confesses, "unlisted. My son was telling me in complete detail about a movie he had just seen, punctuated by three thousand 'You know's?' My teeth were falling asleep. There were three phone calls—strike that—three monologues that could have been answered by a recording. I fought the urge to say, 'It's been nice listening to you.' "

That sets the mood. Like all of us, Bombeck is bored with her life, bored with herself, and bored with her family and friends. She wants a little solitude. She is so tired her teeth are falling asleep, a fractured metaphor that is quite telling. "Strike that," she writes, using the legal cliché for a laugh in the midst of a nonlegal line.

In the cab to the airport, she is assaulted verbally again by the cab driver, who has a son away at college. He's worried about a girl named Diane, who seems to have married his son. The driver never even met her and he doesn't know what kind of girl she is. What is he supposed to do about it, anyway? Suppose he doesn't *like* the girl? And so on and so forth, until Bombeck tunes him out.

Bombeck escapes the driver, gets herself into the airport, sits down, opens up a book, and is happy to wrap herself in her own thoughts.

But it is not to be. The woman next to her is thinking about the temperature in Chicago, which is sure to be cold and damp. As Bombeck tries to ignore her without insulting her, she continues to ramble on.

She hasn't been in Chicago in three years, even though her son lives there, she says.

Bombeck buries herself in her book, pretending it's the most fascinating thing on earth. "That's nice," she says, with that expression that means, "It's anything *but* nice."

The woman goes on, as if she can't stop, telling Bombeck about her husband's body—his dead body! It's on the plane, too, making the flight with them. She's been married to him for fifty-three years; he just died quite suddenly. The funeral director drove both the body and the widow to the plane.

Bombeck is stunned. She can't say anything.

In spite of the fact that she knows she should be a good Christian and *listen*, she can't somehow do it. Even though here is a person simply crying out to be heard, Bombeck is unable to empathize properly. All the woman needs is a listener. She doesn't even want advice, or money, or expertise, or anything that is costly or hard to get. All she needs is someone to sit there and listen to her. It's as simple as that.

But Bombeck can't find it in herself to offer any comments other than a grunted yes or no. She is locked into an inability to communicate.

Bombeck muses that in a country where there is so much supercommunication, it is sometimes almost impossible to find someone who will *listen*.

The woman boards the plane and finds a seat in a section away from Bombeck.

"As I hung up my coat, I heard her plaintive voice say to her seat companion, 'I'll bet it's cold in Chicago.' I prayed, 'Please, God, let her listen.' Why am I telling you this? To make me feel better. It won't help, though."

It's an essay, not a humor piece. Right?

Possibly. But a humor piece is an essay to begin with. The humorist has a point to make. She makes it by producing laughter in the reader or listener. She makes it by producing empathy in the reader or listener, too. Bombeck's piece produces empathy and then sympathy, with the women *and* with Bombeck.

The talkative woman has been an object of scorn for centuries. The gabbling housewife is a stock character out of fiction and drama. Bombeck puts her on scene, sets her up to be squelched and laughed at. But in the middle of the skit, she skews the attack toward a different object. What appears to be a woman who can't keep quiet becomes a human being in desperation trying to keep herself from dissolving into hysteria or grief.

Bombeck becomes the hated antagonist, the target of the assault. Tragedy and comedy present the two opposite faces of the masque; the line between tears and laughter is invisible in some situations.

The twist brings a tear to the eye, not a laugh to the throat. And yet, it is particularly effective because the reader is hooked by Bombeck's method of telling the story.

Chapter 3

Bob and Erma

The Big Man on the Little-Man Scene

If Erma Bombeck owes something to any humorist in the way of inspiration and guidance, that man is surely Robert Benchley. His work, as she once said, formed a most important part of her early reading. The subject matter, the treatment, and the general style of Benchley's material are not substantially different from hers.

It was Benchley who brought the image of the Little Man to full fruition in the world of humor during the 1920s and 30s. More than anyone else he actually set the tone for the type of humorous writing that eventually made Erma Bombeck a household name.

Robert Charles Benchley was born in 1889 in Worcester, Massachusetts, went to Phillips Exeter Academy, and graduated from Harvard in 1912. At Harvard he was president of the *Lampoon*, Harvard's comic magazine. He also participated in the "Hasty Pudding" show as an unforgettable chorus girl.

Benchley's sense of the absurd seemed always to overcome his more conventional instincts. After being given an assignment to write an exposition of how to do something practical at Exeter, he wrote a paper on "How to Embalm a Corpse."

Benchley's humor is shaded with a kind of merry madness, tinged with zany nonsense. He is a past master of the startling non sequitur: "Is life made too easy for the youth of today? Are we raising a generation of pampered dawdlers? What is that on your necktie?"

His type of humor depends heavily on parody and satire, not on one-liners. His pieces are constructed carefully, moving from one level to the next with a controlled precision. If anything, he might be called a low-pressure, understated, droll humorist.

In person, Benchley was a bit on the irrepressible side. "A bland punchinello," he once called himself. When *Current Biography* in 1941 wanted some information about his past for their pages, he sent in the following biography.

He was, he said, born on the Isle of Wight, September 15, 1807, shipped as cabin boy on the *Florence J. Marble* in 1815, wrote *Tale of Two Cities* in 1820, married Princess Anastasia of Portugal in 1931 (children: Prince Rupprecht and several little girls) and was buried in Westminster Abbey in 1871.

"That is not strictly true," *Current Biography* explained in its article on him.

Ernest Hemingway, who knew him well, used to call him "Garbage Bird" as he made his appearance "in the early morning light of Montparnasse" on special occasions. Benchley himself said with some modesty that he was "handsome in an unusual sort of way."

The World of Robert Benchley

There are considerable differences between Robert Benchley's view of life and Erma Bombeck's, especially in what a humorist deals with and how a humorist treats it.

Benchley concerns himself largely with the business world and the man in it. His most famous piece is "The Treasurer's Report." It satirizes, in parody form, the typical muddle-minded prose of the corporate "state of the company."

But Benchley also loves to satirize sports—football games, baseball games, hunting and fishing, hiking in the country, and so on. He was essentially an urban creature.

Anybody Who Hates Dogs and Children Can't Be All Bad

After reading a story by the author of *Little Lord Fauntleroy* about a little girl who reformed a crook caught ransacking her home, Benchley wrote "Editha's Christmas Burglar," in which the "little heroine" tries to reform the burglar and gets herself slapped and tied up as a result.

Benchley doesn't really mock the family as an institution, but he certainly needles its exploiters and sentimentalizers, much in the same way Erma Bombeck does.

"Kiddy-Kar Travel" is an essay on traveling with children.

"In America there are two classes of travel," Benchley begins, "first class, and with children." Travel in Benchley's time referred mostly to travel on trains and not in cars. "Traveling with children corresponds roughly to traveling third class in Bulgaria," he goes on. "They tell me there is nothing lower in the world than third-class Bulgarian travel."

That sets the tone. "The actual discomfort of traveling with the Kiddies is not so great, although you do emerge from it looking as if you had just moved the piano upstairs single-handed."

Benchley refers to travel as "Going on Choo-Choo." "Those who have taken a very small baby on a train maintain that this ranks as pleasure along with having a nerve killed. On the other hand, those whose wee companions are in the romping stage, simply laugh at the claims of the first group. Sometimes you will find a man who has both an infant and a romper with him. Such a citizen should receive a salute of twenty-one guns every time he enters the city and should be allowed to wear the insignia of the Pater Dolorosa, giving him the right to solicit alms on the cathedral steps."

Later, "There is much to be said for those who maintain that rather should the race be allowed to die out than that babies should be taken from place to place along our national arteries of traffic. On the other hand, there are moments when babies are asleep. (Oh, yes, there are. There must be.)"

And so on. The rest of Benchley's piece becomes a scene-by-scene pastiche of various incidents on a train with a fictional "Roger."

When he describes the pleasure of taking a small baby on a train ride as similar to "having a nerve killed," his use of the unvarnished truth recalls Bombeck's description of the atmosphere in a post office as resembling "a clinic for lower back pains." He loves to sprinkle his prose with clichés like "wee companions" "in the romping state"—all gurgly with cuteness—in situations in which the meaning is exactly the opposite. His parenthetical observation about babies sometimes being asleep "(Oh, yes, there are. There must be)" is a recurring Benchley trick.

It is interesting to note in passing that Benchley himself invents names for children and family instead of using the real names of his children. Bombeck does exactly the same thing. She doesn't believe in invading her children's privacy.

Benchly concludes his piece on children "in migration" this way:

"I had a cousin once who had to take three of his little ones on an all-day trip from Philadelphia to Boston. It was the hottest day of the year and my cousin had on a woolen suit. By the time he reached Hartford, people in the car noticed that he had only two children with him. At Worcester he had only one. No one knew what had become of the others and no one asked. It seemed better not to ask. He reached Boston alone and never explained what had become of the tiny tots. Anyone who has ever traveled with tiny tots of his own, however, can guess."

Today's travel with kids does not involve railway travel, obviously. Families travel almost exclusively now by car, or by airplane. But in suburbia many miles are consumed every day traveling with kids in buses. Erma Bombeck sees "Going on Choo-Choo" in a slightly different light. She might call it: "Going on Bussy-Bussy."

But her handling of the subject is quite different from Benchley's. If anything, she takes up where he ends, and develops her theme by studying the subject of how to vanquish the rompers rather than win them over.

"Way up there on my list of 'high-risk professions' is the school bus driver," she begins. "In fact, I consider only two professions more hazardous, high school driving instructors and game show hosts. (Two hosts died this year in a halfway house from terminal happiness.)"

Bombeck does exactly what Benchley might have taught her to do. When she has a chance to insert a joke that has absolutely nothing to do with the subject at hand, she does so: hence, the "terminal happiness" line. In humor, this technique of parenthetical observation is extremely effective, as has been noted. It keeps the main subject from becoming tiresome, and may also produce a bonus smile.

She continues with a fabricated anecdote in the nonsense vein—about an obviously aged woman bus driver who loses her way trying to drive two school kids home and winds up in an adjacent state many miles away from where she started.

When the vehicle runs out of gas, she finds she cannot pay the enormous gasoline bill. Meanwhile, her description is already out on an all-points bulletin for kidnapping.

When the cops arrive at the gas station to take her in for kidnapping, she cries out: "Kidnapping? Me? Cripes' sake, I've already got six grandchildren!"

That winds up the introductory material. Bombeck points out that driving is a skill in itself and cannot be left to amateur volunteers.

The crux of the piece is a parody of the "How I Did It" column so prized by the lifestyle editors today.

Bombeck relates that she has been a member of a highly respected "team"—SWAT (Sedate! Warn! Attack! Threat!)—formed originally to cope with driving an out-of-hand group of fourth-graders to class in school.

When less professional drivers were unable to handle the kids, the SWAT team personnel were called in because of their expertise and experience in "knowing which ones were bleeders and how to make injuries look like accidents."

That last line is really going Benchley's punch line anecdote one step further.

Note in passing a currently effective gag technique: the phony acronym. SWAT really means Special Weapons Advance Team; Bombeck's phony breakdown—Sedate! Warn! Action! Threat!—builds up her upside-down idea of combat. Her line explaining she was one who could "make injuries look like accidents," helps build up the violence and mayhem she advocates—strictly tongue-in-cheek—in controlling children.

Then she continues with a laundry list of wild, antic actions that might happen in a school bus.

• Coping with a kid who can model a slingshot out of a seat belt.

● Handling the youngster who tries to cut the driver's hair out of her ears with scissors while the bus is barreling along at 50 m.p.h.

● Controlling a kid who kicks the back of the driver's seat for miles without stopping.

● Talking a kid down off the sun roof without injuries to any other passengers.

● Stopping the bus so the kid standing on the back seat will spin the full length of the bus.

Too bad. Bombeck reports that SWAT has been disbanded. But there is some serious consideration being given to bringing the team back again.

No question about it, Erma Bombeck is much more militantly up in arms against unruly rompers than mild-mannered Robert Benchley was, except that Benchley's murderous feelings were always lurking just below the surface of his bland prose. Both humorists turn upside down the bland cliché that children are all lovable, beautiful, and marvelous beings who make one's life pleasurable and wonderful.

How to Treat Visiting Children and Stay Within the Law

The principal joke involved in the plot of *The Man Who Came to Dinner* is the guest who accidentally becomes a permanent resident of a household that can't assimilate him. Guests have been subjects of humor through the ages, and both Benchley and Bombeck find more amusement —and terror—in the young guest than in the older, more mature, guest.

"The Stranger Within Our Gates" chronicles the adventures and misadventures of a household invaded by what Benchley calls the "Visiting Schoolmate."

"By this," he explains, "is meant the little friend whom

your child brings home for the holidays. What is to be done with him, the Law reading as it does?"

The visitor usually has a home base somewhere at the other end of the country, Benchley writes. "There's something in the idea of a child away from home at Christmas time that tears at the heartstrings," he goes on, "and little George is received into the bosom of your family with open arms and a slight catch in the throat. Poor little nipper! . . . (It later turns out that even when George's parents lived in Philadelphia he spent his vacations with friends, his parents being no fools.)"

During George's first day he is, according to Benchley, a "model of politeness." But soon all that changes. On day two, at the table, "he announces flatly that he does not eat potatoes, lamb, or peas, the main course of the meal consisting of potatoes, lamb, and peas. 'Perhaps you would like an egg, George?' you suggest. 'I hate eggs,' says George, looking out the window while he waits for you to hit on something that he does like."

After a lengthy discussion, it turns out that he likes only squab and duck. "You toss him a piece of lamb which oddly enough is later found to have disappeared from his plate."

But eating is only a minor inconvenience. "It also turns out later that George's father can build sailboats, make a monoplane that will really fly, repair a broken buzzer and imitate birds, none of which you can do and none of which you have ever tried to do, having given it to be understood that they *couldn't* be done. You begin to hate George's father almost as much as you do George."

And there are still ten more days of vacation!

"And during these ten days your son Bill is induced by George to experiment with electricity to the extent of blowing out all the fuses in the house and burning the cigarette lighter out of the sedan; he is also inspired to call the cook a German spy who broils babies, to insult several of the neighbors' little girls to the point of tears and reprisals, and to refuse spinach. You know that Bill didn't think of these things himself, as he never could have had the imagination."

Later:

"On Christmas Day all the little presents that you got for George turn out to be things that he already has, only his are better. He incites Bill to revolt over the question of where the tracks to the electric train are to be placed (George maintaining that in his home they run through his father's bathroom, which is the only sensible place for tracks to run). He breaks several of little Barbara's more fragile presents and says that she broke them herself by not knowing how to work them. And the day ends with George running a high temperature and coming down with mumps, necessitating a quarantine and enforced residence in your house for a month."

Shades of *The Man Who Came to Dinner!*

In Erma Bombeck's *The Grass Is Always Greener over the Septic Tank*, she covers a similar subject in the chapter section entitled "The Neighborhood Nomad."

In order not to be annoyed at this selection, the reader must accept it from the beginning as a kind of Alice-in-Wonderland story. Nonsense in the style of Edward Lear and Lewis Carroll permeates the piece. There is no logic, no common sense, no *realism* as we know it. It is pure fantasy—really wild stuff, very like the white rabbit, the March hare, and the Red Queen.

The piece starts out with the Bombecks—actually it isn't the Bombecks at all, but the unnamed family that populates the book—realizing one morning at the breakfast table that there are four children there instead of the usual three.

Bombeck begins studying all four faces and realizes that one boy has her husband's eyes, that the girl has her own coloring, but of the remaining two boys, either of them could be theirs or anybody else's.

Finally she isolates the interloper, whom she calls Kenney, since that is the name he gives her.

Upon grilling, Kenney admits that a bit over a year ago he happened into the house to borrow the bathroom, liked the atmosphere of the place, and stayed.

Bombeck hastens to the telephone to talk to Kenney's mother. She tells the woman who answers that she is bringing her son home to her.

Why? the woman wants to know. Has he been bad?

Bombeck drives Kenney to his house and upon entering, discovers that the place is alive with children, wall to wall and ceiling to floor.

Kenney's mother is desperately trying to bring cosmos out of chaos, and failing magnificently.

As Bombeck watches, she realizes a startling thing: not all the children in the house belong to Kenney's mother. They seem to be a random selection of neighborhood kids. She mentions this to the woman.

She admits that none of them is her own. Her Kenney is an only child. Her present charges are kids who feel rejected, who just happened to get lost, or simply came in to see what it was like.

It is because of the constant turmoil in the house that Kenney left, she tells Bombeck.

Bombeck wants to know how she knew where Kenney was. The mother tells Bombeck that she saw his picture on the Bombecks' Christmas card.

As they talk, Bombeck notices that one of her own sons has wandered out of the woman's bathroom. He has been coming to Kenney's house, she learns, to play with some of Kenney's toys!

"If you want to leave him here," Kenney's mother says, "we could use the exemption on our income tax."

Bombeck takes him home.

Pure nonsense, but Bombeck is working a part of the street different from Benchley's. There is a disquieting sameness in suburbia. Bombeck carries the idea to the point of absurdity by creating a household in which the children are indistinguishable from neighboring children. To have an extra child in the house is of course pure nonsense—but only a slight exaggeration for mothers who find neighborhood kids camping in their homes after school, weekends, and evenings.

Bombeck turns the idea on its side in writing about a visit to another suburban household, one in which none of the children belongs there, but in which there are dozens and dozens of interchangeable kids from other homes. The segment is nonsense on the surface, but underneath the jokes sharp satire is at work. Suburbia does produce interchangeable kids; they grow up to become interchangeable adults and to blend into the corporate business structure. Look out!

The Good Queen of Children Everywhere

Benchley's paragraph in "The Stranger Within Our Gates" about the father who can do no wrong has its counterpart in a Bombeck column titled "Everyone Else's Mother." That mother, of course, is the mother who does everything better and is real nice because she lets her kids do exactly what they want.

Note how Bombeck uses the idea to pull off a much more potent assault on children's favorite argument than Benchley did.

She begins her piece by establishing Everyone Else's Mother. Everyone Else's Mother is the one who lets her kids stay up late to watch a movie on television. Almost everything Bombeck denies her own children is a proud possession of Everyone Else, permitted and indeed promoted by Everyone Else's Mother.

Bombeck thinks that this absolute paragon of goodness,

affability, and warmth is simply a product of her children's active imaginations. That is, Everyone Else's Mother does not exist but is simply a lever her children use to bully her.

But then, to her surprise, Bombeck one day meets Everyone Else, the daughter of Everyone Else's Mother.

Everyone Else is no surprise. Bombeck could have invented her if she did not already exist. She is always able to do exactly what she pleases. From the moment of her birth, she always gets just what she wishes. If she wants jelly beans, she gets them. If she wants to ride horseback, she gets a horse. She never has had to make up her bed or clean under the dresser.

Even in school Everyone Else never has to worry. She doesn't have to study. If she is rude to someone, no one catches her up on it. She selects her own clothes, buys as many records as she wants, and is unaccountable to anyone.

Bombeck tells Everyone Else that for years she has heard of her wonderful mother.

"I would *love* to meet her," Bombeck says.

Everyone Else looks at Bombeck in a kid of daze. She frowns, and then repeats the word Bombeck has spoken: "Love?"

"You'd have thought it was the first time she had ever heard of it," Bombeck writes.

Rarely does she put the knife in quite so slickly and so deeply, but when she wields it, she wields it deftly. And the moral is a quickly stated and quickly underlined with that one sentence.

It's a good example of what can be done with a twist of the knife of wit, and the proper wisdom to use it.

"I'm Sorry, You Must Have the Right Number"

The telephone has always been a fitting object of derision—because it is so ubiquitous. In Benchley's early days, much humor was occasioned by the difficulty in getting connected with the proper party. In Bombeck's time, the thrust is somewhat different, as we shall see.

In "The Noon Telephone Operator," Benchley is dealing with live operators, almost completely now replaced by computerized systems. The regular operator is out and a substitute takes her place.

"Let us say that at about twelve forty-five you want to put in a call," he writes. "You lift the receiver and instead of the prompt 'Number please' of your regular operator . . . there is a dead, almost unpleasant, silence. Continued wiggling of the hook results in nothing until, all of a sudden, there is a crashing which sounds as if a heavy body had lurched into a pile of tin pie plates. This is followed by the noise of heavy breathing and a scratching sound as of a heavily mustached lip colliding with the mouthpiece downstairs. Sometimes there is even a bump of front teeth. . . ."

Someone finally says: "Hello!"

BENCHLEY: Wichersham 1259, please.

VOICE: Murray Hill 12593?

BENCHLEY: No, no! Wichersham 1259.

"There is more crashing among the pie plates and then, suddenly, a dead silence, indicating that the machinery has completely ceased to function. . . . More jiggling of the hook brings down more horrendous crashings and heavy breathing."

VOICE: Did you get your number?

BENCHLEY: I'm sorry. No. I wanted Wichersham 1259.

"At this point, the entire switchboard below seems to burst into flames, necessitating the calling out of the militia and dozens of men with fire buckets. The excitement over, there is a slight passage of words between the mysterious operator below and the operator belonging to the telephone company.

VOICE: I want Veeker sam wan—

CENTRAL: Number, please.

Benchley never does get his call through. "And the mysterious part of it is that, as you go out to lunch yourself, there is nobody at the switchboard."

In another account of telephone troubles, titled "One Minute, Please!" Benchley is seated at his desk when the phone rings. "I, in my impractical way, answer it. And what do I get for my pains?"

VOICE: Is this Vanderbilt 0647? Is Mr. Benchley there? Just a minute please!

Benchley waits.

"In about two minutes I hear another female voice."

VOICE: Is this Mr. Benchley? Just a minute please, Mr. Kleek wants to speak to you.

"Remember," Benchley writes, "it is Mr. Kleek who is calling *me* up. I don't want to speak to Mr. Kleek. I wouldn't care if I never spoke to him. In fact, I am not sure that I know who Mr. Kleek is."

VOICE: Just a minute please. Mr. Kleek is talking on another wire.

Benchley fumes. "Now, fascinating as this information is, it really wasn't worth getting up out of my chair for. . . ."

Kleek gets on the wire finally, only to say: "Hello. Who is this?"

Benchley is nonplused. "I am not only to be told to wait until Mr. Kleek is ready to speak to me, but I am to be treated by Mr. Kleek as if I had infringed on his time."

BENCHLEY: Who is this yourself? This was your idea, not mine!

"I hang up so quickly," Benchley concludes, "that the hook drops off."

Nowadays the laugh is not on the operator, or on the instrument, or on the people on the other end—but on the idiot who leases the phone from the phone company.

"We got our phone bill this month and if one more of our kids 'reaches out and touches somebody' they're going to bring back a broken hand," Bombeck begins, mocking the phone company ads.

She then uses several short paragraphs to describe the situation at the Bombeck home. It seems that her children were born with telephones wired to their ears.

She and her husband sometimes walk through the house waving wrist watches and alarm clocks at the telephoners; once Bombeck used a calendar with the date circled in red grease pencil.

Her husband even once suggested that his daughter be sent back to her natural mother—Ma Bell.

Bombeck's phone bill prompts her to initiate a set of rules for placing long-distance calls in the household. The laundry list includes:

● Never place a telephone call without first going to the bathroom.

● Get a drink of water and clear the sinuses before making a call.

● Read the weather report before calling, to eliminate the cliché: "What's the weather like there?"

● Estimate the proper time zone to eliminate the question: "What time is it there?"

● Complete fistfight with brother before dialing number.

● Put the dog outside and let the cat inside before lifting the receiver.

● Laughter takes time; it costs dollars. Save humor until phone call is finished.

● Never repeat needlessly; the response to "I love you" is not "I love you, too," but "Ditto."

● Animals and babies do not bark/meow/laugh/talk until they hear the dial tone.

Bombeck reports that she gave her son the rules and suggested that he not telephone so much, but start writing letters.

"Last night," she goes on, "I heard him reading a letter over the phone."

Oh, well.

Chapter 4

Jean and Erma

What's the Inside of a Car For?

By 1958, when Erma Bombeck was still struggling with diaper rash, exploding sterilizers, and clothes dryers, Jean Kerr had become firmly established as "one of the funniest women writers of her generation."

She had had four plays on Broadway—either as author or coauthor—including *King of Hearts, Touch and Go, Jenny Kissed Me,* and the *Song of Bernadette.* She had written a bestseller titled *Please Don't Eat the Daisies* in 1957. And she and her husband, Walter F. Kerr, drama critic of the *New York Herald Tribune,* had coauthored a new play, *Goldilocks,* which was to open on Broadway in the fall of the year.

In every way she was a contemporary of Erma Bombeck: temporally, environmentally, and psychologically. Three years older than Bombeck, Jean Collins was born in 1924 in Scranton, Pennsylvania—not too far, as the crow flies, from Dayton, Ohio. Her father was a contractor, however, and in her family money was never the problem it was in Bombeck's.

Jean Collins went to Marywood Seminary and Marywood College in Scranton, and in 1941, while working as stage manager at the college for a production of *Romeo and Juliet*, she met Walter F. Kerr, who was at that time professor of drama at the Catholic University of America in Washington, D.C.

Largely because of him, she attended Catholic University for three summers, earning a B.A. degree from Marywood College in 1943. Within weeks of her graduation, she was married to Walter Kerr. Then, two years later, she received the M.F.A. degree from Catholic University.

Jean Kerr's book, *Please Don't Eat the Daisies*, a kind of autobiographical nonfiction novel, appeared late in 1957. It was in part a compilation of a number of pieces she had sold to the *New York Times Magazine*, *Vogue*, *Ladies' Home Journal*, *Reader's Digest*, and other magazines.

It remained at the top of the bestseller lists for twenty weeks. Over 200,000 copies had been sold by mid-1958. "Mrs. Kerr is the kind of woman whose writing is diverting even when turned to so prosaic a chore as a memo to the grocer," wrote Whitney Bolton, of the *New York Morning Telegraph*. John K. Hutchens of the *New York Herald Tribune* called her "a handsome lady with a wit you would have to call deadly."

Metro-Goldwyn-Mayer paid $75,000 for the movie rights and made the picture soon afterward.

The Kerrs had bought a place in Larchmont, New York, where they lived with their sons, Christopher, twins John and Colin, Gilbert, and, later, Billie. Called the "Kerr-Hilton" in the book *Please Don't Eat the Daisies*, the house was originally the stables and coach house of a large estate with turrets, medieval courtyard, and a thirty-two-bell carillon geared to play a duet from *Carmen* every noon.

In the introduction to *Please Don't Eat the Daisies*, Jean Kerr summed up her work habits:

I do about half of my "work" in the family car,

parked alongside a sign that says "Littering Is Punishable by a $50 Fine." The few things there are to read in the front-seat area (Chevrolet, E-gasoline-F, 100-temp-200) I have long since committed to memory. So there is nothing to do but write, after I have the glove compartment tidied up.

Once in a while—perhaps every fifteen minutes or so—I ask myself: Why do I struggle, when I could be home painting the kitchen cupboards, *why*? And then I remember. Because I like to sleep in the morning, that's why.

Kerr's basic subjects are similar to Bombeck's basic subjects: the husband, the family, and, mainly, the kids. Although Kerr's surroundings are essentially suburban, her actual orientation seems much more urban than Bombeck's. She writes about what she knows—seeing shows with her critic husband, throwing parties with intellectuals and creative people in attendance, interior decorating, buying clothes, parodying literature, and so on.

A Terrible Problem in Communication

Although Kerr's smaller subjects tend to be more sophisticated in selection, she uses her children as the main focus of her satire and humor. As does Bombeck.

What she says about kids could easily be said by Bombeck.

"We are being very careful with our children. They'll never have to pay a psychiatrist twenty-five dollars an hour to find out why we rejected them. We'll tell them why we rejected them. Because they're impossible, that's why."

Later on, in a chapter from the book titled *Where Did You Put the Aspirin?* Kerr puts child psychologists under a microscope to watch them squirm. Like Bombeck, she follows all the nuances of the psychological fraternity.

"I'd be the last one to say a word against our modern child psychologists," she begins innocently. "I am prepared to swallow a number of their curious notions, including even the thought-provoking statement that 'children are our Friends.' This premise may be open to question, or even to hysterical laughter, but it probably does contain a germ of truth."

However, she goes on to say, she is unable to admit that children are "really people, little adults—just like the rest of us, only smaller."

Absolutely not, she says, and sets out to prove it by example. The first example is in the simple matter of going to bed. "An adult will say, 'If you want to sit up all night watching an old George Raft movie, okay, but I'm turning in.' And he turns in, and that's the end of him until tomorrow morning."

However, getting a child to bed is a somewhat different problem. After the initial argument about everyone else on the block being up until midnight, she manages to get her son up into the bedroom.

"Now begins a series of protracted farewell appearances. He comes back on the landing to say that his pajamas are wet and he has a neat idea: he's going to sleep in his snow pants. You say it's impossible, how could those pajamas be wet? And he says he doesn't know unless it's because he used them to mop up the floor when he tipped over the fish tank."

Then follows the next skirmish.

"I suppose you want me to brush my teeth."

"Of course I want you to brush your teeth."

"Okay, but I won't be going to school tomorrow."

"Why not, for heaven's sake?"

"Because I'll be poisoned to death."

"What *are* you talking about?"

"Chris used my toothbrush to paint his model car."

After that is settled, the third wave of terrorism begins.

"Mommy, it's raining."

And this leads to the revelation that he has left his bicycle on the lawn next door, and he has tied a "keen foxtail to the handle bar and it will be ruined, just absolutely ruined." With the rescue of the bicycle, the third phase is over.

Then:

"Mommy, this is important. I have to have a costume for the play tomorrow. I'm Saint Joseph."

QED? No way. Kids are obviously quite as able as adults to create terror and panic.

"There are other important ways in which children differ from their elders," Kerr goes on, blithely ignoring the fact that she has not at all proved her thesis. "For instance, it is perfectly possible to have a really satisfactory quarrel with an adult. You say to the beloved, 'Do you mean to tell me that you met Mrs. Gordon and you didn't ask her about her operation? Of *course* I told you, you just don't *listen*. Oh, never mind—you're obtuse, that's all, just plain *thick*!' This should lead to a spirited exchange and result in a good, two-day sulk.

"Conversely, you can tell a child that he's the worst boy ever born into the world, follow up this sweeping statement with a smart thump on the behind, and in two and one half minutes he will come back, look you straight in the eye, and say, 'Wanna hear a neat riddle?' "

There are other differences, Kerr points out.

"Psychologists tell us that the things we *want*, the things we ask for most often, provide us with a vital clue to our personalities. Children, having linear minds and no grasp of the great intangibles, spend most of their energy yapping about trifles: 'Can I have a Coke?' 'Can I have an apple?' 'Can I have a Good Humor?' 'Can I see *Baby Doll*? Dickie says it's a keen picture.'

"In contrast, notice the maturity and breadth of vision that is revealed in this sampling of a typical adult's daily demands: 'Where did you put the aspirin?' 'Did anybody call the plumber about the faucet?' 'Don't you *ever* put cigarettes out?' 'Tell them we can't come, tell them I'm sick, tell them I'm dead, tell them anything you want!' 'Who the hell took my fountain pen?' "

So:

"Let's have no more of this nonsense about children being Little Adults. They are a breed apart, and you can tell it just by looking at them. How many of them have gray hair? How many do you see taking Miltown? How many go to psychiatrists?"

Kerr's technique is to state the theme of the piece—that child psychologists are wrong in believing that children are like adults, only smaller—and then to use examples that prove nothing of the kind.

In fact, in the examples used and in the dialogue, it is obvious that kids are pretty much like adults, only much of the time just a bit smarter perhaps.

Bombeck uses a different technique. She selects a particular idea being espoused by child psychologists, and sets out to put it to the test, with predictable results.

She toys with the idea of togetherness, pointing out to her husband that the family that plays together stays together, or words to that effect. Soon, she fears, the home will be an empty nest and there will be only memories of their children. Now is the time to spend with their loved ones to make the family a more cohesive and affectionate unit.

Her husband is somewhat laggard in his enthusiasm to embrace this new sociological program, but he is willing to humor her. As for himself, he feels that an empty nest will be perhaps a happier nest than the full nest in which he is now crammed.

Quoting the best experts, Bombeck launches into the theme of togetherness, describing the "formative years" when adult and youth exchange ideas and points of view.

In a flash of inspiration, she comes up with a plan. Her husband will take their son on a fishing expedition. Bombeck will spend the weekend in the house with their daughter. Both parents will have one-on-one situations in which they can get into the really "meaningful stuff."

Bombeck describes the touching departure of husband and son, loading up their fishing gear into the car, with the final almost tearful parting. Bombeck goes into the house, enthusiastic about her upcoming meaningful dialogue with her daughter.

But daughter is on the phone, and remains there for what seems to Bombeck to be "more than five hours." She then escapes into the bathroom to take a long shower.

Bombeck, on her knees, begs under the door: "Do you want to talk about anything?"

A faint voice comes back from the shower compartment: "Do you have a clean pair of pantyhose?"

Instead of talk, mother and daughter spend an evening apart. Daughter has rushed out the front door on a date. Their only exchange of information on her feelings about life is a one-way comment by her daughter: "I'm for it!"

After finally rousting her daughter out of bed at noon for lunch and then sitting across from her while she listens to hard rock on a pair of headphones, Bombeck throws up her hands in despair.

So much for her intimate dialogue with her daughter. But when her husband returns, Bombeck's expectations rise. He is smiling triumphantly.

He tells her that he outdid himself. He talked about human values and his philosophy of life. He says he discussed aims and goals; he even explained how a person had to be persevering and patient to get what he wanted. He told his son how to become a man of integrity and honesty and discretion.

Bombeck is amazed. She wants to know what her son told him after assimilating all that.

"Nothing," her husband tells her. "He slept all the way up and back."

Bombeck's treatment is the more obvious. At the end of the experiment she knows the theory is disproved. Or at least she knows that she and her husband were not able to communicate in a "meaningful" way with their offspring. She learns that the offspring don't particularly want "meaningful" communication. They want "a clean pair of pantyhose," "time to phone," "time to rest up in the car," and to listen to music in the earphones.

No self-delusion there.

On the other hand, Kerr sets out to disprove a favorite hypothesis of the child psychologists—that children are just like adults, only smaller—and winds up giving examples which show that they are indeed very similar to adults, even though they are smaller.

Then, to prove the point she hasn't made, she gives tongue-in-cheek examples of "meaningful demands" by adults to compare with "meaningless demands" by children—and totally disproves her own hypothesis that they are different.

The satire here is double-edged; Kerr uses the absurdity of psychological hypotheses to reduce her own psychological hypothesis to an absurdity. She is, in effect, poking fun at herself for misusing psychological tools to try to make fun of psychologists.

Bombeck uses her humor to wage a frontal assault on phony dime-store psychology. Kerr uses hers to flank and attack from ambush, and succeeds in unseating only herself!

There's Something About a Shroud . . .

Jean Kerr is tall and hard to fit for a dress. Erma Bombeck is short and compact and hard to fit for a dress. Both dream of being easy to fit and both dream of being clothes-horses. Horses, perhaps, but *clotheshorses*? Unfortunately, no.

Kerr begins a piece, "I Just Stepped Out of *Vogue*," from her book *Penny Candy*, with an anecdote about seeing a play with her husband in which a male actor turned up in Act Two wearing a dress.

"He was wearing *my* dress," Kerr explains. "I mean the one I had on. There it was, the same check, the same little piqué collar, the same dreary buttons down the front. Except for the fact that I wear my hair shorter and I'm getting quite gray, we could have been twins."

She then relates another incident that occurred when she and her husband were invited to his managing editor's home for dinner. Kerr purchased a dress to wear: yellow silk pongee with metallic gold thread woven through the fabric.

"I went," she writes, "to the party calm in the conviction that for once I was wearing something that did not look as though it had been run up by loving hands at home."

When she arrives at the apartment, they are greeted at the door most graciously. "I felt, however," Kerr goes on, "that the wife's smile was a little bit strained. I understood everything when we walked into the living room. Three walls of the room were covered from floor to ceiling with draperies. And the draperies were made of exactly the same material as my new dress."

Kerr thinks about the situation. "Actually, it didn't matter so much to me that when I was standing in front of a drapery I seemed to be a disembodied head. It mattered more to the other guests, who were hard put to analyze what they assumed must be an optical illusion. . . .

"In fact, one man left my side in the middle of a sentence muttering, 'I don't know *what* they put in this drink.' . . . Needless to say, we were not invited back."

She dreams of not being intimidated by dress clerks in stores, because she always is.

"By contrast, my mother has great authority in these situations. I once went shopping with her when she was looking for a dress to wear to my brother's wedding. The saleslady brought out a somber mauve lace with the ubiquitous rhinestone pin on the hip. Mother waved it away. The saleslady turned frosty on the instant and asked, 'Would you care to tell me what you don't like about it?' Mother smiled cheerily and said, 'My dear, all my friends are being *buried* in that dress.' She got results, and a very becoming gray chiffon, in ten minutes."

Bombeck has trouble with clothes, too, but not the way Kerr does. It's the overall effect she wants to create. She decides she wants to dress for intimidation.

She has studied women and the way they dress to impress one another. There are tricks, she learns, that some women employ to make other women feel inadequate. She wants to learn all these tricks so she can outdo other women and put them down as low as they want to put her down—and beat them to it.

And then she elaborates on her plan.

To her a charm bracelet is a kind of weapon, as important to a woman as a gun to a gangster. She wants to stroll into a room and hear her charm bracelet bong like an anvil whenever she lifts her wrist to down a cocktail.

And she has a throw-away line to utter when everyone looks around at her and goggles:

"I told my husband a typewriter charm with forty-four diamonds on each key was too much, but he *insisted!*"

And in addition to the outsized giant bracelet, she will use an organizer handbag—use it to the hilt—the kind that has a pocket for anything imaginable, and everything imaginable for a pocket.

The big bag can intimidate almost as much as the clattering bracelet can.

But Bombeck can't seem to get the art of snobbery in her stock of clothes. How can she make an impression as a clotheshorse when she walks into a room wearing shoes with a big "G" on the heels, when the "G" stands for Grasshopper and not Gucci?

She recalls her feeling of absolute self-destruction when she meets, face to face, a woman dressed *all in white*. A woman in white is immediately lionized; crowds flock to her like files to a magnet.

"When *her* clothes talk," Bombeck notes, parodying the E. F. Hutton commercial, "everybody listens." To Bombeck a woman in white is putting her thumb to her nose and telling the whole world where to get off.

And a woman in white—*with a hat*—that is *it*. Even a large-brimmed hat, or a veil with an ostrich plume, or a beach straw, or a tennis cap with a visor. *Anything* will do.

But the *real* test, Bombeck feels, where security must exist or everything dies, including the role model, is the way a person dresses on the tennis court. That is the scene where it is possible, indeed highly probable, to intimidate, to flaunt, to rise above everyone and everything.

Bombeck buys herself a tennis dress, a Chrissie Evert pair of shoes, tennis socks with ball fringes on the heels, a racket press. Then—her opponent walks out wearing a sweatband! "It's all over!"

Wasn't That Mrs. Longfellow a Marvel?

Coping with the children is still one of life's main occupations not only for Jean Kerr but for Erma Bombeck, and all other mothers. Kerr's discussion on the subject relies a little more on literary allusion than Bombeck's. But both instantly express their guilt feelings over having normal reactions to the crises of child-rearing.

In "The Children's Hour After Hour After Hour," Kerr descants on the problem in a kind of quiet desperation.

"Clearly other woman have coped better than I can," she writes. "All the time I find myself ruminating about Longfellow's 'The Children's Hour.' If I grasp this poem correctly, Longfellow didn't lay eyes on those kids until sometime 'between the dark and the daylight when the light is beginning to lower.' I take that to be about five-thirty (depending on the time of year). Wasn't that Mrs. Longfellow a marvel to keep those children out of his hair all day long? Remember, he worked at home. I can see it may have been easy enough with Grave Alice. But what about that Laughing Allegra? Can't you just hear her? I'd have been out in the den saying, 'Henry Wadsworth, you watch Laughing Allegra for an hour!' "

It's no problem, Kerr concludes, to love children "when they're being adorable. Even your true Monster Mother (who's never made cookies in her life) is tempted to give hugs to a nice little boy who is drying the silver. And when a three-year-old girl looks in the mirror and says, 'I'm going to be tall and pretty—just like Mommy,' Mommy does not require professional guidance in order to feel loving."

Psychiatrists, she decides, must mean that "you should love children when they are driving you absolutely out of your mind." She then imagines a situation with its aftermath in dialogue as the psychiatrists would wish it:

"Billy, your teacher called. She said you were late for school again. She also said you didn't bring in your homework any day this week, and that you deliberately spilled water paint on Mary Dee's jacket. Furthermore, she said that you constantly disrupted the entire class with your foolish antics. I love you, Billy."

Even Billy, Kerr concludes, would "definitely be rattled."

Bombeck's problem comes in a slightly different guise. All her efforts at sounding off never seem to work.

Fate intervenes, ruining her handiwork. Even sarcasm, that most devastating of all insults, fails.

Her boy is late for dinner. Sarcasm seems the answer: "What's the matter? Get hit by a truck?"

In fact, yes. He was riding his bicycle home when a truck ran a red light. It hit the back of his bicycle and threw him on the road for a few bruises.

Mother's Day arrives. None of the kids appears with a present for her.

Bombeck begins self-pitying speech Number 14A—that eloquent one about sacrifice and dedication. She delineates her family sarcastically as "ungrateful bums," unfeeling wretches. She is beginning to huff and puff a little, showing signs of incipient tears—

The door bell rings. A large bouquet of flowers stands there: MOTHER'S DAY GREETINGS FROM THE KIDS.

Putdown Number Three, which works for anyone else, also fails Bombeck:

"What kind of a boy would skip church?"

Answer: A boy who just happens to be putting out a brush fire near the orphanage at the time.

Even Bombeck's snide remark to her daughter about some uneaten food left on her plate backfires. Muttering something about wasting food while children in Slobovia starve, she elicits this succinct response:

"Mom, Slobovia is a mythical place out of the Li'l Abner cartoon. If you really want to send this asparagus where it will do the most good, try any of the West African nations which are underdeveloped and being subsidized by grain and other foods from all over the world."

But the ultimate failure occurs with her oldest son, who is teaching school in another country. As usual, he fails to write for three weeks. Bombeck makes a person-to-person call and breaks down at the last moment with this fail-safe cliché:

"Why haven't you written? *Is your arm broken?*"

"No, actually, it's my wrist. It's been in a cast for three weeks."

And then the long explanation.

"That's it. I admit defeat."

How Not to Look Like a Rabbit

Both Kerr and Bombeck, like all other women in suburbia, are subject to frequent bombardments of self-help literature. In revenge, Kerr turns out a parody on a keeping-fit article: "My Twenty-One Minute Shape-up Program."

It involves, as they all do, several steps in acquiring a trim body. Detailed instructions come with each step.

For example: "1. Exercise for the Nose. Two minutes. Stand in front of a good mirror. Press your upper teeth down over your lower lip until the entire lower lip is covered with teeth. Lift your nose in the air and wrinkle it until you look rather like a rabbit. Stare at this image for a minute. Now allow your face to relax. You will be forcibly struck with the improvement in your appearance now that you no longer look like a rabbit."

Kerr's example is reminiscent of the old Burns and Allen routine:

"Gracie, why do you keep hitting yourself on the head?"

"Because it feels so good when I stop."

Number two is so close to the typical prose used in fitness articles that it need hardly be rewritten for the parody.

"2. Exercise for Scruffy Elbows. Three to five minutes. (If you can't tell whether or not your elbows are scruffy, ask somebody.) Cut a lemon in half. Scoop out most of the pulp. Heat a little olive oil in a small saucepan. Pour the oil into the lemon cups. Then rest your elbows in the lemon cups. The whole point of this procedure is to give you a little rest. For, while you are actually in the lemon cups, you can't do anything else whatsoever. You can't even file your nails, because the least little jiggling will cause the oil to ooze out all over the table. If one of the children comes in and asks you what you are doing, refuse to answer. For those who worry about such things, I have been assured that this exercise is in no way injurious to the elbows."

Kerr satirizes the ridiculous grimaces and positions such "self-help" exercises require. Both examples are followed by punchlines that are non sequiturs.

Bombeck finds that her physical fitness program involves not only fitness of the body, but fitness of the mind, fitness of the psyche, and so on. She lists the various direct-mail brochures that burden her mailbox, programs which are guaranteed to sharpen her interest in life, challenge all her psychological interests, and enrich her psyche.

1. Sex and Nutrition. Bombeck parodies the typical course by exploiting the obvious question: Do they interact with one another? She includes so-called essential equipment: notebook, pen and—key to the joke—floor cushion.

2. Overcoming Personal Insecurity. Bombeck calls this one "Success for the No-Nonsense Woman." Idea of the course is to teach the go-getter how to give parties, handle interviews, fine-tune speech, dress, makeup, hair, conversation. Bombeck's suggested First Lesson: Walking. She advises participants to wear comfortable shoes.

3. Financial Analysis. Here Bombeck satirizes the adult learning class in stocks and bonds. Value of course: Read the small print and *know what it means!* Also, new tax dodges.

4. Gourmet Cooking. She throws in the usual: foods, herbs and spices analyzed. Learn which foods can be used for medicine. And a rare play on words: "Cook *au na-*

turel"—cooking in the nude? Tag line: "Wear loose clothes," obviously for an after-class feast.

After listing several more like that, Bombeck concludes:

"I don't know. After looking through a couple hundred of these courses, maybe I'll go back to my original goals: World peace and five pounds lighter by Christmas."

Self-help fads are grist for the humor mill anytime. It is hard to keep a straight face while seriously doing the exercises or performing the regimens. Bombeck's recent book, *Aunt Erma's Cope Book*, is a satire based wholly on self-help books. It is discussed in Chapter Seven.

The Magic Eye, Slightly Bloodshot

Although most authors overlook television and try to ignore it since it has no prestige, no literary value, and no enlightening good, it is difficult for the suburban housewife to avoid it.

Kerr confesses that once she became hooked on soap opera. Even though she had always thought of the typical soap opera watcher as "a gin-soaked slattern in her husband's old bathrobe, dirty dishes mounting in the sink, waxy build-up piling up on the linoleum," she fell under the spell quite by accident. "Actually, the gin-soaked part is patently absurd," she writes. "You have to be alert to follow these plots."

However, after spending her afternoons glued to the set, she finally began to invite her friends to attend the dramas with her. And that led to her final encounters.

"My friend Charles, whom I love like a brother, and my brother, whom I love like a brother, both watched with me one afternoon. My brother, rather intemperate by nature, suddenly looked at me in some confusion and exclaimed, 'I don't believe this, you've gone mad.' Charles, who writes for a living (I think that makes him kind of jumpy sometimes), kept shaking his head from side to side and finally muttered, 'Did I hear that line, did I really and truly hear that line?' 'What line?' I asked, honestly perplexed. He was quick to clarify: 'That man on the sofa just pointed his finger and said, "Okay, Dorian, but if Bickie loses this baby she's carrying it'll be on your head." '

"He didn't really like the second program, either. In fact, he seemed to find something humorous in this perfectly straightforward statement: 'I know you don't like Monica, but before you evaluate her personality please remember her skill at fibrillating Mr. Daniels.' Of course, if you're going to be all that picky, you're going to miss a lot."

The satire here is simply critical acumen. Again, like the self-help articles satirized, the actual program is so close to self-parody as to be readily available as humor without much change at all. Kerr's final tongue-in-cheek statement—"if you're going to be that picky, you're going to miss a lot"—makes sense more as a statement of fact than as a critical comment.

Bombeck's war with television has to do with the regular dramatic shows. Her solution is to reverse the lengths of commercials and dramas: extend the commercials and shorten the shows so that they are all about thirty or sixty minutes.

She cites several commercials and points out their extremely exciting dramatic possibilities.

For example, there's the one in which a man comes home to a surprise birthday party. He is greeted at the front door by his wife, who tells him there are a lot of people waiting inside for him.

Then she hesitates, makes a horrible face. She tells him his breath is simply foul. He is embarrassed. She drags him into the nearest bathroom anyway.

A minute later he is wandering around at the party,

breathing on everyone he can, in a kind of antiseptic high. The interest, Bombeck points out, is in what happens the next morning.

Does he stay with his wife? Does he go off with a new exotic partner who falls for his breath? Is their connubial relationship ever the same again? What *really* happens?

Bombeck then pursues the story of Robert Young and Mrs. Olsen, starting out when they meet at a party one night.

Olsen wants to know what Young is doing there, instead of being at home. Young tells her he's at the party because Fred is on the caffeine again.

Olsen says she thinks Fred is mad because he can't come home without tripping over Young's ersatz cups of de-coffee.

Does Young move in with Mrs. Olsen? Does Fred go to Coffeeheads Anonymous?

Bombeck imagines a number of extremely dramatic serials for prime-time television in the various characters in commercials:

The Fruit of the Loom guys. What do they do after hours? Do they have families? If so, what do the kids look like?

The Fluoride Chalk Demonstrator. What kind of baby-sitting jobs does she *really* get? What do the kids think of her two-toned chalk?

The Plumber and His Wife. Do they ever meet anywhere except over a stopped-up sink?

The American Express Card Man. Who's really trying to corner all those travelers checks that keep getting stolen overseas?

As for the big shows, like "Dallas," Bombeck notes that it has a spin-off called "Texas." The teaser goes something like this: "There's only one state big enough to hold all this passion! Texas!"

Bombeck decides that Dallas isn't really the Passion Capital of the world. Where is it?

She runs down a list of famous places where soap operas have taken place: Peyton Place; Knots Landing; Dallas; Denver. Then she runs through some possibilities that haven't been explored. And she remembers her own beginnings in—fasten your seat belts—Cleveland.

Why not? Cleveland—it's "crawling with lust and passion." The place where things are so hot the Cuyahoga River catches fire every summer.

Bombeck mentions that she herself wrote *The Grass Is Always Greener over the Septic Tank* about an Ohio suburb.

Any sex symbols from Cleveland?

Paul Newman was born there.

"Watch for it, folks, soon in your TV listings. . . . 'Cleveland! the only city with enough industrial experience to produce enough sex to keep up with the demand.'"

Chapter 5

Sam and Erma

The Comedian Who Found His Past

In the introduction to *You Don't Have to Be in Who's Who to Know What's What*, Sam Levenson points out that the content of the book—and, consequently, the content of most of his humor—deals with "some of the most serious, often painful, aspects of human existence: love, marriage, family, religion, freedom, war, morality, poverty, wealth . . . subjects that in fact comprise the basic contents of the human comedy."

Levenson deals with almost exactly what Erma Bombeck deals with: the middle-class family, the members of that family, the foibles of marriage, the continuous battle of the sexes, and the general frustrations of living not on a grand scale, but in the little way most of us live.

Sam Levenson came to comedy from that Great Crucible of Humor—the New York City school system. He had no intention of being funny when he was growing up. It was simply something that he caught, like a cold, as he matured.

"Don't call me a comedian—I'm not," he has said many times.

Born on December 28, 1911, in New York, Levenson

was the youngest of eight children—seven boys and one girl—and the son of Hyman and Rebecca Fishelman Levenson.

His father was a tailor who was making about $20 a week. It was his mother, with her tolerant yet firm philosophy of life, who made Levenson see the more cheerful side of living.

He grew up on the teeming East Side of Manhattan in a cold-water flat. His parents always wanted him to be a schoolteacher, because teaching school was an honorable profession. Levenson fulfilled their fondest hopes.

From the beginning, he spent his life among the people he later called the VUPs—Very Unimportant People. It was because he was essentially so normal that Levenson was able in his later years to draw accurately and tellingly on the rich experiences of his early days in Manhattan and Brooklyn. His Very Unimportant People were people who came to be recognized easily by his audiences later in life.

From 1951 to 1954 Levenson was a regular panelist on "This Is Show Business." In the summer of 1955 he substituted for Herb Shriner on "Two for the Money," and appeared once again in 1956.

In 1959 Levenson appeared as a regular panelist on NBC-TV's "Masquerade Party," an identity contest, and appeared on the "Ed Sullivan Show." On "Arthur Godfrey Time," a daily television show, he made several appearances, discussing children and their problems.

Then on April 29, 1959, the "Sam Levenson Show" succeeded "Arthur Godfrey Time."

Meanwhile, Levenson had turned to writing books of humor. These included *Everything But the Money; Sex and the Single Child; In One Era and Out the Other; You Can Say That Again, Sam; A Time for Innocence;* and *You Don't Have to Be in Who's Who to Know What's What.*

God Thought He Could Do Better

The women's liberation movement appealed to Levenson's sense of humor, because it brought a whole new dimension of humor to the eternal battle of the sexes—a war in which Levenson, like all humorists who ever lived, enjoyed participating.

"God made Adam for practice," Levenson writes. "Then he looked him over and said, 'I think I can do better than that,' so he made Eve."

In fact, Levenson understands what women want with their liberation movement—revenge.

"All I want," the woman says, "is the right to sit at the steering wheel in the family car in front of the house at 7 A.M. and honk the horn continuously for a half hour while my husband dresses the children for school."

And on Thanksgiving Day, the woman says: "Let us give some thought to the Pilgrim mothers, for they not only had to endure everything the Pilgrim fathers endured, but also had to endure the Pilgrim fathers."

A couple of other Levenson down-putters of male superiority:

"Any husband who thinks he's smarter than his wife is married to a very smart woman."

"My husband was just named by his college as Man of the Year; which shows you what kind of year this has been."

The eternal female put-down of the male strikes Levenson as funny, too.

"We have yet to see a woman marrying a male nitwit because of his big bust."

Levenson's familiarity and ease with the family environment make it easy for him to understand the women's lib point of view.

"Thank God! I don't have to go to work," the woman says. "I just get out of bed in the morning, and there it is, all around me."

And then, on the other side of the coin:

"The most shocked women in the world are those who get married because they got tired of working."

Levenson also lets the men get in a dig or two at the women.

"A woman's place is in the home. Why should she go out and take away a working man's pay instead of staying home and stealing it out of his jacket like a good wife?"

But the woman has the last word.

"Behind every successful man stands a woman who couldn't manage on his budget."

"Now that I'm working I not only understand economics but can explain it to my husband. A recession is when your neighbor loses his job; a depression is when you lose your job; a panic is when your wife loses her job."

Levenson prefers to use one-liners, even though they may be two or three lines long, to get his laughs. His technique in putting together a book is to include one-liners and introduce them with various types of transitional material. Essentially, each Levenson book is a collection of one-line jokes, but all are grouped into specific categories which can be tied together and compared with one another as he goes along.

Bombeck's technique is pretty much the opposite. She begins her piece with an introductory statement, and then develops the theme in various ways. By the time the piece is finished, she has included a number of one-liners, and perhaps a laundry list or two of items connected by similarity, but she has always kept the main idea of her piece in mind; each segment relates to it.

For example, in one of her columns that might be considered a women's lib statement, she focuses on one aspect of being a woman.

Bombeck announces that she has finally decided to zero in on one of the evil trends in society, one that has been plaguing women in all walks of life for the last two centuries—the ignoble act of having to dance backward.

Tongue in cheek, Bombeck describes it as the real symbol of woman's inferior position in regard to men—a social injustice that has permeated society almost since its inception.

"A woman dancing backward," she goes on, "is like a dog dancing on his hind legs. He does it. But not well."

She then elaborates on her own experiences on the dance floor. Because she has sometimes been in the hands of inexperienced or inept male leaders, she has been pushed into other dancers, into musicians in the band, into chairs, against buffet tables, and even into bananas flambé. In some uncanny way she once found herself at the front of a line into the men's room, and "barely got out with [her] life."

Bombeck quotes one psychological theory about female inferiority as being a surrogate form of pain the woman must bear, akin to giving birth and "skiing with a handbag."

"Skiing with a handbag" is pure Bombeck. It is a tribute to her zany appreciation of total nonsense, the kind of nonsense Benchley loved to get into his images. But anyone who has seen a secretary with a handbag clutched to her waist cleaning coffee grounds out of a coffee maker has a pretty good idea what she mans.

Bombeck reports that she has talked about dancing backward many times with her husband, pointing out how absurd it is, and asking why a woman should always be required to make the sacrifices, but he simply shrugs his shoulders, and says something like: "Sure, it's a rotten job, but who else would do it if you didn't?"

In another examination of the women's lib viewpoint —that is, that the man gets away with things a woman can't get away with—she provides a laundry list of slights men are responsible for:

She starts out the piece asking a theoretical question: Does a man use the same guidelines with his wife in household situations that he uses with other people?

In other words:

● Does he give his wife the same amount of attention he gives Abdul Jabbar?

● Does he give her the same praise he gives his secretary when she moistens the sponge for stamps on his desk?

● Does he listen to her with the interest and attention he gives his garage mechanic?

● Does he give her the protection and love he devotes to his charge card?

● Does he share with her the joy he reserves for a comic page or the office Christmas party?

But there's another side to the coin. Bombeck switches targets to the wife:

● Does she have the honesty with her husband that she has with her gynecologist?

● Is she as enthusiastic for his return as she is when her washer repairman arrives?

● Is she as interested in his day as she is with the menu at Baskin-Robbins?

● Does she have the same pride in his achievements as when she gets the mold off the grouting in the hall shower?

● Does she fuss with her appearance for her husband as much as she does when she visits her safety-deposit box?

Bombeck's one-liners are different from Levenson's. Note that each is a separate punch line introduced by the same lead-in: the lead-in that Bombeck has established at the beginning of the column.

Instead of one answer, Bombeck provides a list of them. Each serves as a joke on its own; all are linked to the same lead-in idea.

It is essential in writing newspaper humor not to waste words; the laundry list of several lines is a technique extremely well adapted to newsprint humor. Like Bombeck, Art Buchwald is a master of this technique.

What to Give a Child Once a Day, Without Fail

Levenson understands children, especially as they operate in the heart of the family. And that includes rearing kids. A good deal of his humor about kids involves the "new" methods of child-rearing. He calls it "the upheaval in the home." The family, he points out, was once "parent-centered."

"The old order," he writes, "ordered corporal punishment for disorderly children. It did not order brutality, but it did teach that sparing the rod spoiled the child."

"Give your child a spanking once a day. If you don't know why," the wheeze goes, "he does."

And: "There were many methods of punishment, but the two most common were backhand and forehand."

Also: "I raised my kids on *Parent's* magazine. Never read it, no; I'd just roll it up and whack 'em on the behind."

One of the old precepts?

"Be a father to your children. If they want an entertainer let them hire one."

And, "What a boy needs is a father, not an accomplice."

But now?

"If you've given up trying to get something open, just tell a permissively raised four-year-old not to touch it."

"There's nothing wrong with a child's behavior that trying to reason with him won't aggravate."

"To have children in their teens is to know that you are living, just as having a headache is proof that you have a head."

Bombeck always has fun with the statistical surveys about kids that pop up in newspapers and magazines. Those dealing with teenage kids particularly interest her.

"Either there is a significant increase in the basic, wonderful values everyone knows and loves so well," she says, "or there is a significant increase in lying."

And she goes on to write about a questionnaire that revealed 50 percent of the teenagers questioned had never had an alcoholic drink; 98 percent had never tried marijuana; 70 percent were virgins; and 53 percent got most of their news from television.

Figures like these drive Bombeck up the wall. She wants to believe the figures, but she can't. Maybe the kids surveyed live just down the block; but maybe not, too. The truth of the matter is, she knows it as well as anybody else: they simply don't exist.

She quotes another survey. In this one, high school students, asked who they would like to be, overwhelmingly decided in favor of themselves—three out of four, anyway.

Bombeck slips in an aside:

"The last time my daughter said that, she was wearing all my clothes, my tennis racket, and my car keys." So much for being oneself.

The high school kids then listed a movie star, followed by a two-way tie—Cheryl Ladd and the President of the United States—and a three-way tie: a millionaire—"that's more like it" Bombeck says—Jaclyn Smith and "my Mom."

Now the questionnaire goes slightly wacky. Asked what they liked to do in their spare time, they came up with: 1. reading; 2. playing; 3. drawing; 4. roller saking; and 5. bicycling.

Bombeck can't contain her astonishment. None of the high school students mentioned *television*. And there was no mention at all of the *telephone*.

The parenthetical observation about Bombeck's daughter who wanted to "be herself" but was wearing most of her mother's best things is pure Erma Bombeck. And so is the parenthetical wisecrack after mention of wanting to be a millionaire—"that's more like it."

In the newspaper Levenson spots an advertisement obviously placed by a housewife requesting paid help. "It sounds as though she has just burned her marriage license," Levenson says and prints his own ad:

WOMAN WANTED; TO HELP IN HOUSE. 18-HOUR DAY, 7-DAY WEEK, SLEEP IN. MUST HAVE KNOWLEDGE OF COOKING, SEWING, MEDICINE, LAW, CHILD PSYCHOLOGY, ELEMENTARY ELECTRICITY, BOOKKEEPING AND SEX. MUST BE STRONG AND WILLING. NO WAGES. ONLY ROOM AND BOARD.

Bombeck has an anecdote that goes a little further. She recalls placing an ad for a babysitter after the birth of her third child when she needed someone to sit with the other two.

"WANTED:" her ad read. "STRONG WOMAN TO SIT WITH TWO ACTIVE CHILDREN. WRITE YOUR OWN TICKET. ORPHAN PREFERRED."

Bombeck says the ad ran for two weeks, without an answer. Then recently, she spotted the following ad that reminded her of hers:

CHILD MENTOR: TO OVERSEE THE HEALTH, RECREATION AND GENERAL WELL-BEING OF THREE CHILDREN. STRESS PRESONAL AND CHARACTER-BUILDING HABITS. ARRANGE OUTINGS, PICNICS, PARTIES AND OTHER RECREATIONAL ENDEAVORS. PLAN AND SERVE PROPER MEALS, DETERMINE BEHAVIOR PROBLEMS (IF ANY) AND TRY TO SOLVE THEM. STIMULATE ACADEMIC INTEREST AND PREPARE LESSON PLANS FOR THE CHILDREN WHILE THEY ATTEND SCHOOL. FREE ROOM AND BOARD PLUS $130 A WEEK.

The ad intrigues Bombeck. But she thinks it's a lost cause. It's either a joke or a stupidity; $1.03 an hour is going to draw either a total moron or someone who has never seen a kid.

The stereotypic image of the babysitter on television amuses Bombeck. She is usually a woman in her fifties, she notes, with some kind of degree in dental hygiene. She carries a piece of white chalk with her which she dips into a green liquid dye to point out the magic of fluoride. When does any babysitter get time to do any chalk-dipping and breaking?

Bombeck's answer to the babysitting problem is to leave a mimeographed list of instructions for her sitters. Included are these recommendations:

"There is a lock on the bathroom door. Use it if you have to."

But the final comment is the payoff:

"Cheer up. You can go home tonight."

Levenson has the last line here:

"Youth is a time of rapid changes. Between the ages of twelve and seventeen a parent can age thirty years."

Brother's Keeper or Keeper's Brother?

Writing about religion is tricky at best, even if you attempt it in a straightforward manner. But writing about religion humorously is almost unbelievably difficult. Most humorists eschew it.

Not Levenson.

"The falling off in congregational attendance ('seventh day absenteeism' they call it), admitted to by leaders of all faiths," he writes, "has expressed itself in troubled humor:

"You must have some sort of religious affiliation. At least your children will know what church you're staying away from."

And if that example sounds too much like a kind of gallows humor relegating religion to limbo, he adds:

"Getting inoculated with small doses of religion prevents people from catching the real thing."

In particular, one sign on a bulletin board near a church, makes him chuckle:

IF GOD SEEMS SO FAR AWAY—WHO MOVED?

Levenson observes that a typical excuse for staying away from church might be:

"I don't go to church because of what they did to me there. The first time they threw water in my face; the second time they hitched me to a nag; and next time they're gonna throw dirt on me."

Levenson not only tackles religion, but politics *and* religion as well.

"We should not permit prayer to be taken out of the schools; that's the only way most of us got through."

Or, as one teacher puts it:

"I know it's unconstitutional, but I always pray before I meet that class."

Mixed with a little sex:

"Now that there's no more praying allowed in school the kids may have to go to motels just to read the Bible."

Levenson sees a card in a wallet saying: "I am a devout Catholic. In case of an accident call a priest." But this one is worn by a nonbeliever: "I am a devout atheist. In case of an accident, goodbye."

And as for the fundamentalists versus the evolutionists:

"The zoo apes are going out of their minds. They can't figure out if they are their brother's keeper or their keeper's brother."

Bombeck generally doesn't write about religion, but she does handle it occasionally. And when she does so, she treats it in an off-handed manner, slightly self-mockingly, slightly self-pityingly.

In Copenhagen, she and her family are looking for a Catholic church in which to attend mass. But Copenhagen does not have a plethora of Catholic churches.

The Bombecks have rented bicycles to go to church. One of their children suggests that dad stop and ask someone for directions to the nearest Catholic church.

But dad demurs; he can't translate Danish anymore than Bombeck can. And she notes, "I only eat Danish and do not understand it."

Finally the group cycles up to a building that resembles a church. The family surveys it but decides that it is closed—an odd thing for a church on Sunday.

The group decides to make a reconnaissance mission into the nearby streets. Bombeck is afraid someone will steal the bicycles. Her two sons volunteer to guard them. Bombeck suspects their motivation is evasion, not security.

So does the head of the family. "We are all going to mass and pray together for love and forgiveness," he says, "if I have to break some heads to do it."

Eventually they locate a church. It is definitely not Catholic. When they enter they find no holy water, no confessionals, and no statues of Mary.

Bombeck tries to move into a pew past a parishioner. It is a wino dead to the world. At this moment a man dressed in black with a white ruffle around his neck appears. He gives the sermon. It is in Danish.

He walks down toward the Bombecks, paying no attention to them, but lifting the wino's wrist to take his pulse. He seems pleased. The Bombecks thank the pastor for his sermon.

Once outside, a citizen staggers over to Bombeck's husband and pulls out a bottle of beer, offering him some. Bombeck is horrified; she thinks for a moment that her husband will take it.

They get on their bikes and peddle back toward their hotel. "The family that prays together," Bombeck concludes, "gets on each other's nerves."

Note that Bombeck treats the churchgoing sequence

more as a travel anecdote than a straight-on confrontation with religion. She avoids religious discussions or remarks because she feels her audience doesn't like it any more than she does. She too, like Levenson, senses that in today's secular society, many people—her children included—tend rather to avoid going to church than to attend regularly.

Workers of the World, Unite!
... Workers ... Workers ... Workers ... ?

"One of the key values that have suffered serious deterioration in our recent civilization is the work ethic," Levenson writes.

In olden days, fathers taught their offspring to work. "Learn to handle a tool, and you will never have to handle a begging bowl."

But that was a long time ago. Today, the work ethic is, if not dead, very retired and possibly vanishing from the face of the earth. This leads most people to avoid it like the plague.

"They say hard work never killed anyone," Levenson writes, "but why take a chance on being the first casualty?"

"Maybe hard work won't kill a man, but on the other hand who ever heard of anyone resting to death either?"

An indifference to work and a lack of craftsmanship have contributed to sloppiness and slovenliness through every stratum of society.

"Some people are so good at learning the tricks of the trade that they never get to learn the trade."

Here's a builder's instructions to his contractor:

"We don't want the building to collapse, so don't take away the scaffold before you put up the wallpaper."

And, on a more grisly, black-humor note, a wanted ad:

"WANTED: Man to Assemble Nuclear Fissionable Isotopes, Molecular Reactivity Counters, and Three-Phase Cyclotronic Uranium Photosynthesizers. No experience necessary."

Levenson notes that ambition, initiative, and inspiration are rare today, rare enough to cause old mottoes and precepts to be altered:

"Early to bed and early to rise makes a man healthy, wealthy, and wise," now comes up as: "What can you expect of a day that starts with getting up in the morning?"

Even Aesop's Fables are updated:

"Once upon a time there was a lion so ferocious that he ate a bull. He felt so great that he roared. A hunter heard him roar and shot him.

"MORAL: If you are full of bull, keep your mouth shut."

Bombeck reports on the death of the work ethic in a much more realistic and, somehow, more ruthless, fashion.

She gives the younger generation no quarter, beginning her piece by stating flatly that all children are spoiled today and have been pampered from the moment of birth.

The girls don't know how to cook, have never, as she puts it, "seen a chicken naked without benefit of seasoning or dressing." The boys have never bothered to learn what makes up a simple Waldorf salad.

Once, she recalls, her son witnessed the making of a Caesar salad: the garlic, the lemon juice, the oil, the Parmasan, the Worcestershire Sauce, and the raw egg floating in the bowl.

He turned pale at the sight. "Gross!" he muttered, walking away.

Revenge is sweet, Bombeck muses. The kids are grown up now. The phone is constantly ringing. One time it is her daughter, desperately demanding answers and quickly. The big question is: *how do you make spaghetti?*

The phone rings again. It is another offspring. There is

a native curiosity here. The potatoes in the pantry are beginning to put out shoots. What does it mean?

Bombeck visits one of her children and happens to open the refrigerator. A half container of yogurt sits on the first shelf. A roll of film and a petrified lime sit on the second. There is a doggie bag in the egg keeper, later identified as Sweet and Sour Pork.

Bombeck runs out into the living room crying out that there is absolutely nothing to eat in the house.

"Don't believe what you hear about revenge being empty and meaningless," she chuckles. "It was wonderful!"

It's Not Easy to Avoid Being Born

There is a fallacy that life is a constant joy and surprise. But not everyone really believes that.

"It's better not to be born at all," Levenson quotes the pessimist. "But who has such luck? Maybe one in a million."

Getting older is a problem, too. It's healthy to have bad health once in a while, but no fun.

"Some people say they'd like to go to bed at night healthy and wake up dead in the morning," writes Levenson. "Not me. I'd like to linger, to linger and suffer and linger and suffer and go to doctors and bigger doctors who won't know what's keeping me alive, and then linger and suffer and linger, and, then, the last minute, I get all better."

Bombeck finds aging a deadly drag. Even the milestones in her life prove to be crashing bores.

Reviewing her life year by year, she makes note of the expectations and of the realities, and comments.

For example, she recalls that all her elders had promised her great things when she finally reached the age of twenty-one. It was to be her "best" year.

Bombeck points out that when she reached that age, she was unable to finish college. No funds. She was not going steady; in the words of her mother, she was "the only girl in the country without a boyfriend."

At thirty there were more promises. The idea was that she would always be wanting to look back on her life at thirty—great years!

She was married then, her husband was working from dawn until dark. The baby was in orthopedic shoes that cost a fortune and had to be replaced every twenty-one days. For her birthday present, she wanted long finger-nails and a dinner ring. She settled for a hot-water heater. She had to save up for three months to frost her hair.

Then at forty, another milestone:

Worse. Now she was beginning to sense the intimations of mortality. She was spending thirty dollars to have her hair colored. She was using Erase to take out the wrinkles. She was resting after lunch to let her food digest. And the spookiest thing of all: she always seemed to be seeing her mother's hands coming out of her coat sleeves.

At fifty? She had it made? Sit back, relax, and enjoy it? No way. That year, the Bombecks installed a revolving door in the house for the returning children. She could only afford dresses that came in one side—size ten.

Bombeck won't let the hypocritical theory that aging is a lot of fun prevail without a fight. She uses the old un-varnished truth technique to reveal aging for what it is. Also apparent is the exaggeration of her statement that she was the only girl in the country without a boyfriend. Later on, the complete fizzle—a water heater for a birthday present. The image of her mother's hands coming out of her coat sleeves is a triumph, a way to say her hands were aging *without* saying it. And the final exaggeration: "I ate lunch and had to rest while it digested."

Both Levenson and Bombeck have similar approaches to much of their comic writing, because essentially they are both satirizing the middle-class family. And both really love family life, in spite of its rigors and its many unbearable problems. There are a warmth and a love, but each sees the flaws and the drawbacks clearly and tries to correct them in his or her own way.

Chapter 6

Art and Erma

The Master of Adulterated Rot

Although Art Buchwald writes a thrice-weekly humor column on the same schedule as Erma Bombeck, he writes about a slightly different middle America from Bombeck's. A large percentage of Buchwald's columns are political in intent and in content. Others deal with such male-oriented subjects as sports, business, and recreation.

Nevertheless, although dissimilar, the Bombeck and the Buchwald columns are in many ways alike—in technique, tone, and general style. The devices of humor are the same: the hyperbole, the nonsense, the current names, the dialogue.

Not only do their columns frequently share space in certain newspapers, but the authors also share a good friendship. Bombeck is the only female member of the exclusive American Academy of Humor Columnists, a "nonpartisan, nonprofit, and otherwise nonexistent organization" that hands out awards to each member and encourages the exchange of funny memos.

It was Buchwald who, along with another newspaper humorist, Russell Baker, originally founded the organization. In addition to Baker, Buchwald, and Bombeck—how the *B*s predominate in American newspaper humor!—there are two other working members. One is Art Hoppe, columnist of the *San Francisco Chronicle*. The fifth member is Gerald Nachman, who began a humor column for the *New York Daily News* in 1973, and then dropped it.

When Russell Baker won a Pulitzer Prize in 1979, Buchwald fired off a memo to the members of AAHC accusing Baker of having spent $100,000 to lobby for the prize and suggested a response to any queries about the award should be: "I have no comment until I read one of Baker's columns."

Baker immediately sent back an answer by wire thanking his colleagues for planning a "gala testimonial dinner" in his honor. "Unfortunately, I cannot accept," he added, "as I will be busy throughout the rest of the spring counting my prize money."

This exchange led Bombeck to note that "if we put as much effort into our columns as we have into our correspondence, we'd all be millionaires." Bombeck was kidding; she is at least a millionaire once-over already.

On a bookshelf in Buchwald's office is a picture of Baker, an old Washington friend, with the inscription: "To Art Buchwald, who with Lyndon Johnson and Richard Nixon was all that made Washington worthwhile for ten long years."

What to Do with Bare Navels in the Classroom

The big controversy over the teaching of sex facts in schools, quite an important public issue in the 1960s and 70s, appealed to Buchwald's antic sense of humor. Like Bombeck, he tackled the problem immediately in one of his columns, facing the problem head-on:

"There is a big flap going on in the United States right now over the question of teaching sex education in our schools .... I usually like to stay out of controversial matters since I hate to answer my mail, but in this case, I have to come out for teaching sex education in the schools.

"This is a very personal matter with me. I had no formal sex education when I was a student, and everyone knows the mess I'm in. If there had been a Head Start program in sex education when I was going to public school, I might have been a different man today."

Buchwald loves to dabble in the empty double meaning. The statement about the "Head Start program" making him a "different man today" is typical; it hints at something quite risqué, but upon examination, it is empty nonsense.

"When I was going to Public School 35 in Hollis, New York, we got all our sex education at the local candy store after three o'clock. The information was dispensed by thirteen-year-olds who seemed to know everything there was to know on the subject, and we eleven- and twelve-year-olds believed every word they told us.

"Some of it, I discovered later on, did not necessarily happen to be true."

Like Twain and every other humorist before him, Buchwald loves the understated truth, as in the foregoing. Then he elaborates:

"For example, I was told as an absolute fact that if a girl necked with you in the rumble seat of a car, she would automatically have a baby."

Leading, of course, to the remark:

"This kept me out of the rumble seat of an automobile until I was twenty-three years old."

Buchwald has a genius for setting up a mythical situation, expanding it, extending it into an absurdity, and then compounding the absurdity by pretending it to be true. Without knowing Buchwald has his tongue in his cheek, the reader becomes a witless victim of his humor, much like Hagerty was in the Eisenhower incident.

Buchwald continues the piece by explaining that when he turned thirteen, he and his contemporaries became the "teachers" of the younger kids, even though they did not know any more then than they did before about sex.

Thus, he is able to posit his conclusion:

"So, on the basis of my own experience, I don't think we have much choice in this country when it comes to sex education. In order to avoid the agony and pain my fellow classmates and I went through, we either have to teach sex in the schools or close down every soda fountain in the United States."

The satire is double-edged. Buchwald is, on the face of it, advocating sex education in the schools. But at the same time, in detailing the manner in which he and his peers learned about sex by "instruction" he is also ridiculing the use of such "instruction" in the classroom. By the time the reader has finished, he guesses Buchwald is pulling his leg in two directions at once.

Bombeck handles the subject a bit differently in *Grass*, under the heading "Getting Sex Out of the Schools and Back into the Gutter Where It Belongs."

The segment begins with an interview between Bombeck and her son's teacher. The teacher is quite upset over the Bombeck boy's limited knowledge of sex, in particular of the reproductive organs.

The teacher cautions Bombeck about her son's lack of knowledge. He thinks, she tells Bombeck, that "fertilization is something you do in the fall to make the lawns green."

Under severe questioning, Bombeck admits that she has never really discussed the parts of the body with her son—except for those that show dirt the most.

Shaking her head, the teacher lectures Bombeck on the modern world. Sex is nothing to be ashamed of, she points out. Young people must be informed about the body and its parts; about sex and procreation. For example, she tells

Bombeck that she herself is pregnant and that she told the class all about it.

"You've got one in the oven?" Bombeck says with surprise.

The teacher is shocked at Bombeck's old-fashioned euphemism as well as at her lack of sophistication. She points out that openness and candor are a must in today's world. Sex must be more out in the open.

Bombeck then shifts the scene in the narrative to a meeting of parents at the high school to discuss the future of sex education.

The crux of the problem, it seems, is the dress code at the school. And the problem of the dress code seems to be the visibility or the invisibility of "the navel."

Note that Bombeck is fusing all the sex symbols into the navel—using the navel as a kind of euphemism for breasts, thighs, legs, and so on. Because she has chosen the navel to exemplify all sex characteristics, the hush-hush talk about the navel becomes part of the joke itself.

The "discussion" among parents at the school meeting is a mixture of strained comments, weird euphemisms, misunderstandings, and shocked reactions.

One flustered parent thinks that all this open sex is forcing the children to grow up too fast. That will mean that kids get acne at ten and that their voices will change at nine. That's much too fast, even for today's world.

"Let's save the navels for later when they can handle them and enjoy them like adults."

That's putting it on the line. By using the navel as a euphemism for the complete arsenal of sex, Bombeck has scored her point.

Before the meeting breaks up in a shambles, a vote is taken and the dress code in which navels must be covered is passed, to the relief of most parents.

Bombeck's treatment of the problem of sex education is more cutting, more direct. She satirizes unmercifully the typical use of euphemisms in parental discussions of this kind. The use of navel—probably for *all* sex organs—is a beautiful ploy. The "concerned mother's" concluding statement becomes a double entendre that sums up the ridiculous coyness of the discussion.

We don't know how Bombeck really feels about sex education, but we do know how she feels about parental meetings about it, and about her teacher's advocacy of it.

The Moth That Was on a Diet

The foibles of people are always grist for the mills of the satirist. During the monotonous demonstrations on U.S. college campuses several years ago, Buchwald took aim at and pierced the hypocrisy and Alice in Wonderland logic of college leaders.

"One of the things that impresses people about the students' demonstrations," he begins, "is the strong stand that some members of the faculty take on the issues."

The first sentence contains the key phrase: "strong stand." Most faculty members did *not* take strong stands. Buchwald indicates his point of view by speaking with his tongue in his cheek from the start.

"I was on the campus of Northamnesty University and ran into a professor who was trying to stop his nose from bleeding," he goes on. "His clothes were torn up, and he was walking with a pronounced limp."

Buchwald asks him what happened.

"The militant students just took over my office and threw me down the stairs."

Buchwald is sympathetic. "Why that's terrible!"

"From *my* point of view it is, but I think we have to look at it from *their* point of view. Why did they throw me down the stairs? Where have we, as faculty, failed them?"

Buchwald is confused by the logic.

"There was one heartening note," the professor goes on. "As they threw me down the stairs, one of students yelled, 'It isn't you, Professor. It's the system.' "

"That must have made you feel better."

"As I was tumbling down, the thought did occur to me that at least there was nothing personal in it."

"Nothing personal" is a catch line from *The Godfather*, uttered at the time an enforcer is killing a transgressor. Buchwald mixes both ideas together for the proper comic effect. The entire scene is upside-down. The professor is apologetic for being maimed.

Suddenly Buchwald notes that the students on the quadrangle are erecting a scaffold. "They wouldn't hang anyone, would they?" he asks uncertainly.

"They haven't before," says the professor. "But it's quite possible that this is their way of seeking a confrontation with the Establishment."

A group of students run up and grab the professor. "We got one here," one student yells. "Get the rope."

"Don't worry, Professor," Buchwald shouts as he is pushed away by the mob. "I'll get the police."

"I wish you wouldn't," the professor says as the students drag him toward the scaffold. "If we don't let the students try new methods of activism, they'll never know for themselves which ones work and which ones are counterproductive."

Total madness, total anarchy, total irony. Buchwald, a genuine liberal, doesn't let that fact blind him to the idiocy of the student demonstrations and their empty purpose. Nor does he condone the hands-off attitude of the faculty members during the time of turmoil.

His satire points out devastatingly the illogic of the faculty member in making self-blame a torch to carry, when the blame for the unrest should be placed directly on the students. It is not hypocrisy Buchwald is unmasking, but self-deception.

As Buchwald unfrocks the sentimentalists, so Bombeck unfrocks the pollyannas of society. One of her characters is Candide and Pollyanna rolled into one. What sets off Bombeck initially in one column on hypocrisy is the total duplicity and unmitigated mendacity of a politician during an election.

In particular, it amuses her that the politician who loses somehow puts such a good face on his loss that it *appears* to be a win. The idea is that if the candidate gets only 5 percent of a certain district, and his opponent gets 95 percent, the 5 percenter will smile and point out that his 5 percent vote is a "real breakthrough"—the idea being that since the district *belongs* to his opponent, his 5 percent is 5 percent *more* than he deserves.

Bombeck calls that "depressive winning."

But it isn't only the politicians with their public relations tactic of best-face-possible-on-a-bad-situation that bothers Bombeck; she is annoyed as well by people who live in the "best of all possible worlds"—while Bombeck lives in *this* dirty old one.

As she exudes self-pity and moans morosely about her fate, she definitely and absolutely does not want anyone else trying to cheer her up!

But Bombeck's Pollyanna epitomizes phony optimism. Pollyanna—Bombeck calls her by another name—is never saddened by the sight of a dead tree, or an Out of Gas sign. She always sees good.

If someone complains about her washer being on the fritz, Pollyanna has an upbeat answer: "Thank the Lord it wasn't on a weekend!"

Other Pollyannaisms:

"My husband went out for pizza Saturday and never came back."

"At least he didn't ruin your whole week."

Or: "The rabbit died."

"He probably had no family."

Voltaire knew how to sink in the shaft. So do Buchwald and Bombeck. There are better things in life than always smiling. There's crying, and screaming, and just plain sulking.

The Four-Year Paper Chase

College is no joke to the parent who must pay the bills. Yet the college student is the target of every humorist who has ever come down the pike. The particular slant of the satire varies from generation to generation.

In the past it was the rah-rah aspect of college: the hip flask, the raccoon coat, the patent-leather shoes. Later it was football, proms, and partying at all hours. Then the entire scene changed. Colleges became hotbeds of demonstrations. After the demonstrations were over, rules and regulations went out the window, particularly those regarding the sexes. College became unisex. One big sex orgy after another. So it was said.

Buchwald sensed the absurdity of the situation. In "Oh, to Be a Swinger" he talks with a young student who has a very special problem.

"My parents are coming up next week, and I don't know what to do," the student tells him. "I told them I was living off campus with this coed in an apartment. But the truth is that I'm living in the dormitory."

"That shouldn't really disturb them," Buchwald says.

"Oh, but it will. They're very proud of me, and they think I should have a mind of my own. When Dad heard I was living off campus with a coed, he doubled my allowance because, as he put it, 'Anyone who is willing to spit in the eye of conformity deserves his father's support.' I don't know what he's going to say when he finds out I used the money to buy books."

There's the upside-down situation in a nutshell: the

father will be angry his son spent his orgy money to get a little learning! Then Buchwald zeroes in on the popular press.

"*Life* magazine," says the student, "in a 'Sex on the Campus' article, made it sound so easy to find a coed to live with. Well, let me tell you, for every girl who's playing house with a male college student, there are a million coeds who won't even do the dishes . . . . I asked ten girls if they wanted to live with me. The first one said she didn't come to college to iron shirts for the wrong guy, four told me frankly that it would hurt their chances of finding a husband, four told me to drop dead, and one reported me to the campus police."

Buchwald suggests the student tell his father he can't introduce the coed he's living with because she's going to have a baby.

"Hey!" the student responds. "That's a great idea. I might cause Mom to cry again, but it will make Dad awfully proud."

The satire of Buchwald's column is double-edged. It not only cuts through the campus idiocy of "open dorms" and the "unisex" lifestyle, but puts some of the blame where it should be: on the media for distorting the problem in the first place.

The payoff line is a bit of a gem. In the upside-down atmosphere of the current social mores, the father will be proud that his son has overstepped the bounds of morality.

At no time is there any mention of education, except in the backhanded remark that the student is afraid his father will be unhappy he has spent money on buying books.

Bombeck presents the college situation in a slightly different light, but the barbs are as sharp. Her target is the educational product itself—the "wisdom" one acquires at college.

"My son graduated from college last week. As he swayed down the aisle looking for the world like a Supreme Court judge who needed a haircut, I couldn't help but reflect on the wisdom he had amassed in four years."

The image of the Supreme Court judge in need of a haircut is pure Bombeck at her best. But there's more in her laundry list of fantastic "insights" into life that her son has acquired at college. She divides the list up into the four years.

In his freshman year he learns a very good lesson, according to Bombeck: that classmates who owe money tend to drop out of school before the year is out to "get in touch with their feelings" in some natural hideaway like Big Sur.

In his sophomore year, he learns another lesson: that wearing a car makes a man taller, wittier, and more attractive than wearing old sneakers.

Also: that a checkbook requires a course in mathematics, not a course in creative writing. Deposits must exceed withdrawals.

In his junior year, he learns an even more important fact: that an occasional communication with parents makes them think they're getting their money's worth out of sending him off to college.

In his senior year, he is finally beginning to get an insight into life. He knows that eighteen unpaid traffic tickets can stand between a man and complete success in the outside world.

Also: that a note from the college library, sent to the home, demanding that *Erotic Dreams and What They Mean* be returned immediately or else young Bombeck will receive a blank diploma, can throw both mother and father Bombeck into cardiac arrest.

At the windup of the column, Bombeck concludes: "I cannot remember what he got the degree in . . . but he looked older and wiser somehow."

A Place to Get It All Together

A vacation is supposed to be the time when a hard-working husband and a hard-working housewife can get together and go somewhere to share a few days or weeks without the cares of the world hanging heavily on them.

That's what it's supposed to be.

But vacations are not quite what they seem, as any humorist knows. Buchwald knows what to do, but when he gets there, it isn't quite what he thinks it is supposed to be.

"Whenever I get discouraged about the world situation," he writes, "I go to Martha's Vineyard, that lovely isle of green off the good Cape of Cod. Here people have learned to live in harmony and peace, and everybody gets along with everybody else, and with only a few exceptions."

Naturally enough, we know that everybody *doesn't* get along with everybody else, given Buchwald's ironic tendency to write with pen in cheek.

His first encounter is with a fellow in a drugstore. "Can't stand the people on the mainland," the drugstore habitué says to him as the two drink malted milks next to each other.

Buchwald is apologetic. "Don't blame you."

"You rent or own?" the man asks Buchwald.

"I rent."

"I thought so. You look like someone who rents."

Buchwald is appalled. "Does it show?"

"Certainly. People who own can tell people who rent a mile away. We don't have much use for people who rent."

"I'm thinking of buying," Buchwald says lamely.

"Where?"

"In Vineyard Haven."

"Low class of people buy in Vineyard Haven. Hardly anybody worth knowing lives there."

"There are a lot of writers who live in Vineyard Haven."

"We don't think much of writers around here. They're always taking ads out in the newspaper and writing letters to the editor trying to change things. . . . You sail or motor?"

"Does it make any difference?"

"You must be joking. People who use sail hate people who use motor. We're trying to banish motorboats from the island."

"I like to sail," Buchwald pleads.

"Ketch or catamaran?"

"Do I have to make a choice?"

"Yup. Ketch people have no truck with catamaran people."

Buchwald gives up. "You would think on a little island like this everyone would work together and love each other."

"They make much better malted milks in Chilmark," the man says, looking ruefully at his glass.

"If you don't like it here, why don't you go back where you come from?" Buchwald cries out in anger.

"I used to live in Menemsha, thirteen miles down the road, but I had to move here because of my sinuses. People in Menemsha don't like people with sinus trouble. It gives the town a bad name."

Buchwald titles his piece "Getting Away from It All." The satire is pointed and almost painful. The common stereotype of the kindly crackerbarrel sage in some remote area of the country is turned upside-down to make him an obvious bigot of the worst sort, the kind of hate-thy-neighbor boor who points up the narrowmindedness and meanness of the small towner.

Buchwald's rejoinder, "If you don't like it here, why don't you go back where you come from?" is a beautiful snapper; a neat shifting of the cliché from the deliverer to the recipient.

The dialogue establishes a continuous pattern once it starts. Everything the friendly visitor says is immediately denounced, denied, or contradicted. Even when the visitor tries to agree with the native, he is denounced. The insults become even more pointed when the visitor tries to be nice. A statement of total simplicity becomes a challenge to the native.

Nothing the visitor can say works. Even when he turns on the native and denounces him in uncharacteristic anger, the native refuses to be denounced, pointing out that he *can't* go back where he came from.

Obviously, Buchwald's haven is *not* the place to "get away from it all."

Bombeck handles the vacation situation quite differently. In fact, her main argument is that what's good for the goose isn't necessarily good for the gander.

"My husband's idea of a fun vacation is sitting around watching a ranger pick his teeth with a match cover," she starts out. Obviously she doesn't think much of the mountains. "My idea of 'roughing it,'" she goes on, "is when you have to have an extension for your electric blanket."

In the yearly squabble with her husband over where to go on vacation, Bombeck opts once again for the Big City where she can go to the theater and visit all the shops and department stores.

Of course, her husband opts for the mountains where he can enjoy the camping, hiking, and fishing. That type of activity Bombeck disdains as watching "mosquitoes hatch their larva." She says she doesn't want to stand around at what she calls "Murk Lake" watching men "shave out of double boilers."

Bombeck's husband has a few choice words about the New York stage—he says he doesn't care to watch naked actors running around on a platform.

More argument. In the last analysis, there is the usual: total impasse.

The Bombeck comic images are good: "watch a ranger pick his teeth with a match cover," and "watch men shave out of double boilers" both hit the nail on the head.

Then Bombeck comes up with a laundry list of recreational desires:

- She wants to be able to sleep in a bed where the alarm clock is on the opposite side.
- She wants to be able to lock herself in the bathroom and know that when she looks out through the keyhole she will not look into another eye.
- She wants the phone to ring—for *her*.
- She wants to walk into a room and find all the drawers closed.
- She wants to be able to drink a cup of coffee while it is still hot.
- She wants to be able to pick up her toothbrush and find it dry.

But when she gets to New York, it isn't like vacation time at all. She doesn't have the same experience as Buchwald, but she does have a problem:

As the two of them stand on the corner of Forty-second Street and Seventh Avenue, she sighs with rapture. It is, she says, the first time in years that husband and wife have been away from the house without the children. They are free! At last they can do exactly what they want to do, no strings tied.

Her husband says he wants to find a restaurant where he can get lunch.

Bombeck likes the idea. She takes his hand and helps him across the street, warning him to watch out for drunken drivers who might try to run a stop light.

In the restaurant Bombeck immediately begins to choose his food for him. He tries to restrain her, but she won't listen to him. She warns him about the dirty food and suggests cheese or peanut butter sandwiches because they're harder to ruin.

Then she directs him to the men's room. "Don't sit on the seat," she tells him, "and don't forget to flush."

Once he returns he finds she has cut his sandwich for him. When he points out what she's been doing—treating him like a child—she admits she's simply a creature of habit.

They discuss their next move. Now that they're free of the encumbrance of children, Bombeck has it all planned out. With the whole week free, they're going to go somewhere and shop—for something for the kids.

The satire here is very obvious and pointed. A woman's idea of getting free of the children isn't at all the same as a man's. The more Bombeck is away from her kids, the more she thinks about them. Her husband can't escape either because he's with her. In fact, he becomes her child, and she his mother. Force of habit.

The joke is in their inability to relax and enjoy themselves, even though they *are* alone and free.

The American Woman Has the Right to Know

Mark Twain was the one who made the much-quoted comment about the weather: "Everybody talks about the weather," he said, "but nobody does anything about it."

The same can be said about sex morality: everybody talks about it, but nobody *does* anything about it.

Buchwald imagines a meeting of the editors of a family magazine called *Perfect Happiness* at which a financial crisis is being discussed.

"Our circulation figures are down," one of the editors says. "Housewives are turning off on us by the thousand."

Another says, "Our problem is that we're a magazine devoted to the home, and the magazines that are selling these days are those devoted to sex. Our readers would never stand for our discussing sex in a family magazine."

The art director gets a bright idea. "They wouldn't stand for it if we came out *for* it, but what if we had an issue devoted to coming out *against* it? Suppose the theme of the issue is titled 'The Sexual Revolution Is Ruining America'?"

The executive editor is all for it. "We could say we feel it's our duty as a leader of the mass media to show the American mother what dangers await her children in a permissive society."

"Right. We could get offensive still pictures from *I Am Curious (Yellow)* and *The Killing of Sister George.*"

The discussion continues with other suggestions: "*Hair,* showing those horrible nude bodies on the stage"; "photographs from *Che,* the Off-Off-Broadway show they closed after one performance"; "a montage of all the dirty-movie advertisements"; "salacious passages from *Portnoy's Complaint, Couples,* and *Myra Breckenridge*"; "aphrodisiac foods and the dangers of them"; "the topless look and the bottomless look, and how fashion designers have destroyed the clothes industry."

The editor knows how to balance it up. "We'd have to have some articles from respectable people who are as shocked about the sexual revolution as we are.

"All we're doing is showing the horrors of the sexual revolution. We don't want our readers to get any enjoyment out of this issue. Our slogan is still 'You May Not Like It, But the American Woman Has a Right to Know.' "

Buchwald's comments are so close to the truth that parody is unnecessary. The column might have been a tape-recording of a magazine staff discussing an issue on sex. The cynicism displayed by the editors is so natural that it is almost unnoticeable. That points up the satire Buchwald is after.

Bombeck handles the same situation from the standpoint of women.

Like men, women tend to be hypocritical about sex even when they are talking among themselves.

Bombeck sets up a scene in which a group of neighbors discuss a "house of pleasure" discovered in their very suburban neighborhood. A madam vacated the premises along with her girls as soon as her avocation was revealed.

The neighboring wives discuss the situation among themselves, voicing their disgust at the presence of such a house in their respectable neighborhood. It should be torn down, one says; then she won't have to stand at the window all day and check out the cars.

Another admits that she never would have suspected it was there had she not happened to get a glimpse of the place through a hole in the hedge.

Another states that nothing could ever get her *near* the place.

They all agree something should be done about it; it's a disgrace and a calamity to the neighborhood.

"What would you say if I told you I could get a key," Bombeck asks.

They all cry in unison: "We'd *kill* for it."

This is Bombeck at her most pointed. Each of the women speaks in the veiled moral tones suburbanite women use in conversation. At the same time, several statements belie themselves. One woman who pretends ignorance has obviously clocked all the cars that drive up. Another has observed the house for hours through a hole in her hedge. When these paragons of morality find that they can get inside the house, they rush to the scene.

The rest of the column describes various kinds of adornments in the place: zebra-skin bar; jacuzzi; steam room; chiffon curtains; soft music; shag carpet "that went to your knees"; massive stone fireplace; mirrors everywhere; and a large round bed, swathed in red plush velvet.

Bombeck's punch line: "The sign on the front yard read, 'By Appointment Only.' It figured."

Hypocrisy, especially sexual hypocrisy, has always been the target of the humorist. In today's ultra-sex-oriented society, the hypocrisy sometimes becomes even more pointed.

The men in Buchwald's piece are actually exploiting the hypocrisy which they know exists in the women in Bombeck's column. Often those who cry censorship most loudly are those who most enjoy inspecting the forbidden fruit to make sure it is salacious enough to merit suppression. They are also consumers of what they call "smut" and "porn."

Chapter 7

Bombeckiana Revisited—II

Erma Bombeck's Nine-Inch Shelf of Books

It is small wonder that politicians, personalities, sportsmen, and world figures of all kinds love to become authors of books. The prestige of a book is immeasurable, and the prestige that accrues to its author is an ego trip in itself. Even if the book fails to become a bestseller, the fact of material in print between hard covers makes the person whose name is on the product a kind of "big name," a person of importance, a success.

Yet except for the occasional bestseller, the writer of a book is one of society's lowest paid slaves. H. L. Mencken's description of a writer as an "ink-stained wretch" holds true even more in today's inflated economy than it did in recent years of prosperity—with the obvious exception of the handful of writers who produce blockbusting bestsellers.

For the newspaper or magazine writer, a byline on a book is a seal of approval. Newsprint is notoriously short-lived. Today's newspaper column is tomorrow's garbage wrapper. With the newspaper humorist, the lifetime of a laugh is even more short-lived. Today's joke is tomorrow's cliché.

Not surprisingly, therefore, Erma Bombeck yielded to the appeal of collecting her columns and publishing them in book form. After all, she had already written them. Assembling them and packaging them with amusing chapter titles and subtitles was easy work at best. Illustrator Loretta Vollmuth added line drawings to set the humorous tone.

Her first book was called by the name of her three-times-a-week column: *At Wit's End*. Although the sale of the book, published by Doubleday in 1967, was not sufficient to propel it into bestseller status, its publication did put Bombeck on the map. It enlarged her audience, embracing many women who read mostly library books and lived in areas of the country where her column was not printed, including some metropolitan areas.

It also helped get her name around the television talk shows. It helped publicize her on the lecture circuit. Contrary to what many people may think, writers of books go on the lecture circuit not to supplement income derived from the sales of their books, but to earn money to *live* on.

On a television show Art Buchwald recently snorted in amusement at the fallacious assumption that his column revenue and his book sales pay his bills; it is, he said, his *lectures* that make him the money, in some months bringing in many times the revenue of his printed efforts. Writers of prestige novels and intellectual tomes are forced to do the same thing to hustle up bread.

The publication of *At Wit's End* was an enormous leg up for Bombeck the humorist. Reviews were few and far between, but she did become established as a humorist with a national reputation.

The *Library Journal* review, written by Suzanne Lennon, said: "Erma Bombeck is a syndicated columnist who writes humorously of the small, everyday events in the suburban housewife's life. In *At Wit's End*, apparently drawn from her columns, she takes up the '. . . six predictable depression cycles that beset a woman during a twelve-month space.' She depicts the problems, frustrations, and loneliness that afflict any women in this affluent age. Although this subject has been discussed exhaustingly in the last few years, Mrs. Bombeck's flippant, irreverent style with many clever metaphors and similes, should provide a few chuckles from the harried housewife.''

Publisher's Weekly included a review in its "Forecast" section: "Columnist-wife-mother Erma Bombeck describes her book as a 'group therapy session' to cheer up depressed housewives. Mrs. Bombeck humorously re-creates the moments when the kids—or their father—are about to be *really* too much, the discovery of a figure that isn't what it used to be, intellectual stagnation, recreation and holiday hysteria, . . . women's club meetings, the children growing up, etc. The author—whose syndicated column appears in sixty-five newspapers—is usually funny (though sometimes it's a strain); now and then she is serious or nostalgic. Bombeck is both and housewives are going to approve of the combination.''

The reviews are correct: the book itself is simply a collection of her early columns, without much rewriting or organizing other than lumping them together into subject categories for the semblance of order.

But the benefits of publication were amazing. More newspapers subscribed to her column. She found herself in greater demand on the lecture circuit, although her family situation made her hold down her appearances to a half dozen a year.

The book did fairly well, but it was no rocket. The editors at Doubleday knew that it would be risky going along with another collection of columns from her as followup, so they suggested that she team up with Bil Keane, a syndicated cartoonist whose shtick was satirizing the middle-class family, as Bombeck's did, but from a male point of view.

In 1971 the Bombeck-Keane book was published. *Just Wait Till You Have Children of Your Own*, like *At Wit's End*, did modestly well, but was not a bestseller. It did get a few reviews, but made no great splash in the publishing waters.

Publisher's Weekly tended to be negative. "A look at Erma Bombeck, columnist for the *Dayton Journal-Herald*, with illustrations by Bill [actually Bil] Keane. This is superficial generation-gap humor that should reassure Middle America. The kids Mrs. Bombeck writes of seem scarcely to be into drugs and politics. What are they into? Orthodontia, phone marathons, unisex dress and hair, sibling rivalry, love affairs in cars, sex education, TV and rock—although regarding the last, one isn't sure Mrs. Bombeck has touched base, since she calls Joan Baez a rock star.

"The humor is that of a harassed but gallant suburban parent who may be closer to the old *Saturday Evening Post* covers than to the kids."

The Kirkus Service, an outfit that criticizes newly published books for the library buyers, slammed it.

"Passably humorous palaver about parents and teenagers—the hair, the telephone, the lovelife, clothes, the works. Isolated lines have a frayed charm and keep you reading on: 'If the good Lord had meant for you to wear bell bottoms, he'd have flared your ankles.' But they're few and far between the snappy Roz Russell retorts and the strained banterings. A mini-amusement based on that nonextant stereotypical kid."

Both reviews actually miss the point. It is the collaboration that is unsuccessful. In fact, the book seems to be the kind of property that never really understands what it is. In most books of humorous prose, the illustrations are used to elaborate on the words the author has written.

Gluyas Williams's classic illustrations for Benchley's books are quiet and subdued and yet give added belt to Benchley's barbs.

Keane's background was mostly in magazine and newspaper cartoons, single-panel jobs with funny captions. His work had appeared in slick magazines of all kinds.

The prose and pictures in the Bombeck-Keane collaboration seem to be fighting with each other. Most of the cartoons are separate gag ideas, with original captions. To give some semblance of organization to the book, a group of Keane cartoons, complete with captions, are thrown together with one or two Bombeck columns to create a subsection; this segment is then given a title like "Sibling Bill of Rights" or "Telephone Fever."

Then, because these sections are so small, they are in turn lumped into larger segments, resembling chapters, titled with more gag titles like "How I Discovered I Was Living with a Teenager," "Theories I have Blown," and "Stone Age Versus Rock Age."

The columns themselves are full-blown Bombeck. The cartoons are perfect Keane. But the way they are assembled somehow seems to destroy the package.

The results of the collaboration were apparently not encouraging to the editors at Doubleday either. When Bombeck's next book came out in 1973, it was once again basically a prose offering, containing many of her columns, with a few illustrations by a woman artist named Loretta Krupinski.

The gag title was good: *I Lost Everything in the Post-Natal Depression*. But the book is not really about child-bearing. It is rather a hodgepodge of items that first appeared as columns. For example, the book contains eight longish chapters that may or may not be expanded column ideas, or may or may not be combinations of various columns, along with five more "chapter" groupings of a dozen-odd regular columns lumped together by subject matter under clever chapter headings.

The eight long chapters have some fine gag titles —"Ironed Sheets Are a Health Hazard," "I Gave Him the Best Year of My Life," and "She Has a Cold. Shoot Her"—and so do the combination chapters, including "Put Down Your Brother, You Don't Know Where He's Been," "We Have Measles . . . It Must Be Christmas," and "40 Anonymous."

"Erma is a spokeswoman for those millions of house-bound, children-chasing, food-fixing women who are too busy living and giving to *be someone* or *do something*," wrote Shirley A. Smith in the *Library Journal*. "In this latest expanded collection of items from her syndicated columns 'At Wit's End,' she writes in the tongue-in-cheek style of Jean Kerr and Betty MacDonald, giving sometimes insightful, always humorous comments on the current middle-class suburban lifestyle. A truly wise and funny woman; a laugh-till-you-cry book for public libraries."

Publisher's Weekly saw it as a "housewife's complaint by the popular syndicated woman's page columnist who carries wit and hyperbole to the nth degree. Mrs. Bombeck's discernment of the ghastly trivia that drizzle endlessly on the suburban housewife, especially on a loser, is joyous in its precision and rightness. Through thirteen chapters she embroiders the eternal themes: the foibles and fallibilities of hubby; a woman's day—cooking, shopping, bringing up kids; neighbors; marriage in sickness and health; Christmas shopping. . . . The woman who'll buy this book knows nothing's a non sequitur when everything leads to everything else."

"This is no Class A Number 1 out-of-control housewife we have here," wrote Pamela Marsh for the *Christian Science Monitor*, "but a deliberate comic who doesn't place a foot or a word wrong without deliberate intent."

Doubleday was happy enough with the package to order a first printing of 70,000, quite large for the average humor book. But Bombeck's audience was growing, by leaps and bounds.

The Story of Centerville, Ohio

The three books she had done were successes, at least in general sales. However, Bombeck wanted to do more. She wanted to write a kind of suburban *novel*, a story about settling in the suburbs and coping with the many problems of life there, and not just a volume of funny ideas with no cohesive link.

Apparently Doubleday wasn't interested in the project. The company seemed satisfied to put out collections of her columns, illustrated and humorously titled. Bombeck decided to pitch her idea elsewhere, at McGraw-Hill, for one. In 1974 the company gave her the go-ahead to try her "humorous novel" of suburbia, and she started in.

Later on, kidding a *New York Times* newswoman, Bombeck revealed that she was inspired to write the book after reading James A. Michener's bestseller *Centennial*, a novel about the settling of the West.

"I really thought suburbia was the last great frontier," she told Judy Klemesrud. "I thought about how people got into their stationwagons and shouted, 'Stationwagons, ho!' Of course I didn't go as far back in history as Michener did—I just went back to the Welcome Wagon lady."

Klemesrud took it all down, recording that Bombeck spoke "in a tone that was about as serious as her book."

Bombeck worked hard at her work in progress. "I'm a very disciplined writer," she said in discussing the writing of her fourth book. "When I do a book I work seven days a week from 8:30 A.M. to 3:30 or 4:00 in the afternoon." And she works on her column at the same time.

It took her about a year in between her columns to get the manuscript ready. She turned it in to the publisher and it was approved. Its original title was to have been "As the Tupperware Turns," she said in an interview. However, she went on, the Tupperware people got upset.

"Then we thought about 'Confessions of a Girl Scout

Cookie Pusher,' but the Girl Scouts didn't like that. Then it came upon me that the septic tank people aren't militant, and so that was it."

The title: *The Grass Is Always Greener over the Septic Tank.* "The characters are based on people I used to know," Bombeck said, "and the town is based on Centerville, Ohio, where I used to live."

When asked if the title of the book was a true statement—that is, that the grass *is* really greener over the septic tank—Bombeck responded:

"It sure is. Moisture and goodies come up through the soil. One woman told me she even started the plants in her garden over her septic tank. I told her I'd never eat a salad at her house."

In 1976 the book appeared. It was a great improvement over her first three collections. There is a narrative thread that, however tenuous it is, holds the story together and gives it a semiconventional story line. But the real advance concerns the writing itself, the tone, the feeling.

The thrust of the satire is much keener and more penetrating than before. Not only the usual suburban problems—minuscule annoyances at best—are included (crabgrass, high taxes, and teenagers), but bigger ones as well, including the conformity of life, the restrictions on individuality, the focus on status and money. All these and other, even larger problems are put under the microscope, some viewed tentatively, others thoroughly.

"She manages with the deftness of a trapeze artist to come up with a smile on her face in the midst of unaccountable maneuvers," wrote H. T. Andrews of *Best Sellers,* January 1977. "She takes her joy and strength from the things she satirizes—we need more of that!"

However, *Library Journal,* which had previously applauded her books with enthusiasm, now turned against her. "Bombeck's humor is aimed at pointing up the absurdities of the suburban American, middle-class life-

style, with its timing; its real or imagined 'necessities,' "
wrote J. W. Powell, who went on to complain that the
author's humor had become diluted by overexposure in
newspapers and on television.

In spite of *Library Journal*'s reservations, the fourth
Bombeck book hit the public where it lived, and it quickly
became a bestseller that got to the top and remained on
the lists for nearly a year. It sold over half a million copies
in hardcover alone.

By now Bombeck had become a complete success. But
she had other irons in the fire, irons that now became hot
enough to be shaped into greater success.

Erma Bombeck's Coast-to-Coast Caper

The publication and subsequent success of *Grass* brought
all kinds of good things to Bombeck. The money from the
book was substantial. She got a great deal more coverage
by the media, print and electronic, because of its success.
There were articles in magazines about her. Everything
was coming up roses rather than grass.

One of the roses was a chance to appear on ABC-TV's
new "Good Morning, America" show as a regular. The
morning network program debuted in November 1975.
Bombeck appeared in a twice-a-week slot on the show,
which was designed in a magazine-type format with interviews, feature stories, and shorter "column-type" segments.

Bombeck refused to move to New York to appear live
on the show, which was hosted by David Hartman and
cohosted by Nancy Dussault. A remote production staff
was set up, allowing her to film two segments each week
in Phoenix.

After several months of shakedown many of the other
projected regulars on the show had been dropped for one

reason or another. Bombeck survived, hanging in there in her original format.

Actually the bridge from print to live in the humor business is no novelty. Humor of the kind in newspaper columns is essentially oral. When Robert Benchley began his original humorous pieces, he used parodies of speeches as his medium for comedy. He actually delivered these pastiches in front of college audiences. Print was simply a means of carrying the material to a larger audience later on.

Therefore, it was no surprise that Bombeck's forays into television on the "Good Morning, America" show were successful from the start.

Reviews of the Bombeck routines on the "Good Morning, America" show were uniform in their approval, but varied in their qualifications.

"Erma Bombeck was funny enough in her housewife as humorist role, which may be rewarding if some real housewives get a high out of it," said the *Baltimore Sun*.

The *St. Louis Globe-Democrat* had no criticism of Bombeck herself, but was generally negative about the show. "The laugh-track accompanying Erma Bombeck's commentary wasn't needed. Phony laughs are bad enough on prime-time comedies. At that hour of the morning, they are sickening."

C. W. Skipper of the *Houston Post* said Bombeck was "a very funny woman." "I'd be happy just to sit there and chuckle when Bombeck is on, but ABC has seen fit to give her what I'm sure is a laugh track in hopes of stimulating laughter. Or else she has a small audience of friends and neighbors who seem to laugh on cue.

"Bombeck also seems used to working with editors, and I don't believe ABC has given her one. I don't think some sentences came out exactly as she intended.

"One came out this way: 'How can I keep a bathroom clean with children?' What she intended to say was something like, 'If I have children around the house, how can I keep a bathroom clean?' "

The *Washington Star-News,* writing off the "Good Morning, America" show as a "kind of low-brow *Reader's Digest,*" liked Bombeck's "sharply focused routine" but hated the "canned laughter," which raised the question in the viewer's mind of how it got into her living room in the first place.

The Bombeck routine caught on. The canned laugher was dumped and the segment stood up well without it.

Within weeks she had picked up hundreds of thousands of new fans—many of whom went out to buy her book and improve its status as bestseller.

In adapting her material from print to television, Bombeck varies her style of comedy but little. A script for a two-and-a-half-minute bit is, of course, shorter than an ordinary daily print strip. But the material and the way it is handled are the same. Some of her appearances on television seem to be simple readings of her columns, as indeed they are intended to be.

Sometimes, however, she varies her approach and actually gets over into a visual type of humor. In a recent stint on "Good Morning, America" she interviewed a hog at a farm using hogs to investigate diet patterns in human beings. Bombeck traveled to the hog farm, discussed the situation with a scientist there, and then gagged an interview with one hog.

In another segment, she did an entire skit without any words except for the initial theme-setter. "They say girls are neater than boys," she began, and then performed the rest of the segment in pantomime, showing the cliché to be untrue. The camera examined each piece of junk as she pulled it out from under her daughter's bed, from behind the dresser, under the blankets, and so on, with each object good for a smile.

Mostly, Bombeck delivers her monologue in her own

inimitable low-profile style, front-on to the camera. Dressed neatly, but not flashily, in the attire of the typical suburban housewife, she discourses on food blenders, automobile jargon, jogging, and so on. Occasionally she slips in a serious piece, as she did just before one Christmas; the tenor of the piece was that without young children around, Christmas is more sad than happy.

Although most of the reviews on the "Good Morning, America" show were favorable to Bombeck, not everyone was enamored of her. In a followup evaluation of her stints on the ABC-TV show, Frank Rich, of *Time* magazine, wrote in 1978 that her appearances were "one of the most depressing spectacles on television," and went on to assail her presence and her persona.

"She delivers her one-liners in a strident vibrato; she luxuriates in canned laughter as though it were the praise of a Nobel Prize jury." To sink in the barb and twist it some, he concluded: "Bombeck used to satirize the vulgarity of American suburbia; now she epitomizes it."

In spite of such criticism, the segment on ABC-TV's "Good Morning, America" is still going strong after four years, on Mondays and Wednesdays.

On a Color Set the Grass Turned Brown

Things were beginning to swing for Bombeck and her ever-growing legion of fans. With her immediate acceptance and accelerating popularity on network television, coupled with the fact that she was the bestselling author of a hot property, it was inevitable that Hollywood would take a look at the Erma Bombeck phenomenon.

Coincidentally, Carol Burnett, whose CBS prime-time show had finally run out of steam, was being canceled at just about the time *Grass* became a bestselling institution. Where better to put Burnett's not inconsiderable talents to work than in the Bombeck hot property? Teamed with John Grodin and Alex Rocoo, Burnett was signed up to play the lead in a television adaptation of the Bombeck book that was to be broadcast in prime time as a made-for-television movie.

Bombeck was not given the chore of writing the television script. It was assigned to two writers who had won Emmy awards, Dick Clair and Jenna McMahon. The script they turned out was written in such a way that it could be adapted to serve as a pilot for a weekly series, if the subject proved popular enough. There was big money in a series; much more than in a single shot.

The show was broadcast October 25, 1978, on CBS-TV at 9 P.M. EST. A reviewer in St. Petersburg tried to talk to Bombeck by phone about the show before it was aired. But she was too busy to chat with him.

"I had to settle for watching a preview of the movie," he wrote later in the *St. Petersburg Times*. "I crawled back to the office doubled up in laughter. Nobody better articulates the American woman than Erma Bombeck."

He told his readers that the show was an adaptation of the hilarious story of a city family that moves to the suburbs. "The movie sticks relatively close to Mrs. Bombeck's book of the same name." Writing that she did not do the script but that it was assigned to two other writers, he said "they did a fine job of creating continuity from Mrs. Bombeck's one-liner jokes."

Carol Burnett, the critic said, "is at her best." "There are some truthfully humorous sketches within the movie on being visited by an insurance salesman, having a house party, and spraying the dog for fleas."

However, the St. Petersburg reaction was not shared by everyone who saw the show. Frank Rich, at *Time* magazine, loathed the thing. Part of his animosity was directed in print not at Burnett, who played the lead role, but at Bombeck, for the story on which the show was based.

He pulled no punches. The best thing about the television play based on her book, he wrote, was that she herself did not play the heroine. "That odious chore has fallen instead to Carol Burnett, an actress who is often capable of extracting humor from even the most puerile material. This is one of her rare failures."

Then Rich turned to attack Bombeck again. "Bombeck's stale jokes about crabgrass and Tupperware parties defy levitation; the cutesie plot is predictable to anyone who has ever encountered any incarnation of *Please Don't Eat the Daisies.*"

Standing Behind Bill Russell in the Parade of Life

By the time the fiasco of the Bombeck television pilot occurred, her fifth book had been published and was on the stands for about half a year. As soon as she had completed *Grass,* she had gone ahead on its successor, tentatively titled, she told one interviewer, "Life Is a Parade, and I'm Standing Behind Bill Russell." Actually, that was only a "working title," if indeed it existed at all except as a puff gag.

Bombeck's fifth was, instead, titled *If Life Is a Bowl of Cherries—What Am I Doing in the Pits?* The occasion of its publication was a far cry from the absence of fanfare that greeted her first effort. Bombeck had been featured in a *Life* profile in October 1971, but except for a followup interview in the *New York Times* after she had been on the bestseller list for some months, there was little Bombeck public relations copy in print. There had been, of course, excerpts from her books in several of the bigger women's magazines. But there was little about her as a person.

Now, however, on the strength of her previous showing, plus her twice-weekly stints on ABC-TV, she began to get the treatment usually reserved for show-biz personalities.

In January 1978 *Newsweek* ran a one-page piece on her titled "The $500,000 Housewife." After extolling the bestselling exploits of *Grass*—500,000 copies in hardback sold—Diane K. Shah mentioned her upcoming television special starring Carol Burnett, reminded readers she appeared twice weekly on television, and pointed out that *Cherries* would be out in April.

In addition, Shah said that paperback rights to *Cherries* had just been sold for $1 million. To celebrate, the story went on, the author uttered a typical Bombeckism: "I didn't do my laundry for three days."

In February, *Ladies' Home Journal* ran a special article by Bombeck on women's rights. It was not a humor column as such, but a stronger article on feminism.

In April, *Good Housekeeping*, for which she once used to do a regular monthly column, assigned Phyllis Battelle to write a profile on her for the magazine's article section.

Herbert Mitgang was detailed by the *New York Times Book Review* to run a story on Bombeck's newest book in April.

In May, *People* magazine did a treatment on Bombeck, casting it as a question-and-answer interview in which it reported that *Cherries* had already "vaulted to No. 2 in its second week on the bestseller list." Asked if she felt at all like a television celebrity—which by then, of course, she was—Bombeck responded: "No. I'm a one-woman show. I do my own makeup. I sweep up and vacuum. But for someone who was never recognized by her butcher when she got the next number, this is a really big thing for me. I never get over the shock of someone recognizing me."

In September, *Book Digest* ran a seven-page interview with Bombeck, tape-recorded by editor Martin L. Gross.

In October, *Ladies' Home Journal* ran an excerpt from a book called *Beginnings*, by Thomas C. Hunter, in which Erma Bombeck's story, "How I Made It to the Top," was featured. The excerpt was Bombeck's story.

This was print-medium hype of an astonishingly extensive kind. It helped keep *Cherries* on the bestseller list. In addition, Bombeck was everywhere on the talk shows flogging the book.

The reviews, which hit the newsprint in April, were fairly good. Even the sophisticated big-city *New York Times* took a stand on her for a change. An editor of the *Times Book Review* and onetime author, Richard R. Lingeman, gave her a fairly balanced review.

"Her style is a bit hectic and slapdash, sounding as though she scrawled the column on the back of a laundry list while stirring the evening's Hamburger Helper," Lingeman wrote. "It's the kind of style that is a half beat ahead of her readers, giving them a twitch of recognition and the feeling, 'I might have written that myself.' The columns, later thriftily basted together to make a book, seem just right for the women's pages, in between the recipes and Heloise's Household Hints and feature on 'How to Tell If Your Cellulite Is Malignant.' "

After a rundown on typical Bombeckisms, Lingeman ended: "So one is left admiring Mrs. Bombeck for giving voice to a segment of the population that is not always heard from, but the trivia of whose lives may be, on the higher scale of things, as significant as anything that takes place in the male or sophisticated or urbane world. There is truth in the best of her humor, as well as sanity; what it lacks is the lift and play of language and wit. Sometimes she serves up a meat loaf extended with empty gags; even home cooking can pall, if not relieved by the occasional soufflé."

Other critics were kinder. "In her syndicated column, Bombeck likes to picture herself as a frowzy, inept, frustrated, catastrophe-prone housewife," wrote *Publisher's Weekly*. "She is, of course, a sharp and very funny lady, and her latest collection of sketches is generally right on target. . . . In this collection, Bombeck casts a merrily jaundiced eye on the 70s scene, advising the reader how to survive the tennis craze, to detect a spurious picture of glamorous career women who double as super haus- fraus, to cope with the thought of premium offspring liv- ing in coed dorms. She is less successful when she waxes sentimental—several sketches verge on the maudlin. But her satirized description of family relationships will prob- ably captivate the same audience that enjoyed *The Grass Is Greener over the Septic Tank*."

Some of the reviews were not that kind.

"Erma Bombeck is a very funny woman—sometimes," one newspaper critic wrote. "After a while, though, her essays all seem the same and her humor is lost through repetition. That is why she is better as a newspaper col- umnist than as a book author."

Nevertheless, the critic approved of her writing gen- erally. "Individually, most of the essays are bright, witty, imaginative, and fascinating. Yet all too often the book bogs down because every essay relies on the same type of motherhood, wifedom, and semiserfdom humor that has made her one of the most famous female humorists around today."

After a list of some of her anecdotes, came the conclu- sion:

"And most of the essays are really pretty funny. But much of the humor is lost if the book is read in long sittings rather than in a piecemeal manner. The same downbeat humor is threaded through every section of the book and most of the jokes become predictable by the third or fourth chapter. If the reader is a busy person who picks the book up at odd moments throughout the week to read a chapter here and there, it is a coup for Mrs. Bombeck and an exceptionally humorous event for her fans. But if it is digested in one gulp, *If Life Is a Bowl of Cherries* . . . will leave the reader with an empty feeling in the pit of his stomach. It isn't bad, but it sure doesn't stick to your ribs."

And yet some newspaper critics loved it: "Bombeck . . . is delightfully outrageous in many of her reflections and suggestions. Most of this new volume is a catalog of laughs, snickers, and guffaws. But she closes out this latest work with several short pieces that reflect a depth many readers may not have realized she had. In one, she paints a loving, yet realistic and poignant portrait of her own aging mother and that crucial turning point where roles are switched, when the child becomes the keeper.

"In another, and one that will hit very close to home for parents whose children have just reached the point of leaving home, she muses about Christmas and the 'chimes' she heard when she received a gift of love rather than material value. Now, too many gifts are glossy and shiny and 'silent.' "

In conclusion, "Nothing can ever quite remain the same, but Bombeck, in her native genius, makes sure that it isn't forgotten. She makes us feel good about ourselves and reveals the importance of the everyday individual. Highest recommendation."

Best Sellers wrote: "Fourteen chapters cover the gamut of marriage from its beginnings to old age. . . . The survival manual dealing with replacing toilet tissue, washing toothpaste off side of washbowl, turning on stove, closing door, turning off light, and operating clothes hamper will appeal to all mothers and even old-maid aunts. . . . A delight to read!"

The *Kirkus Review* said that Bombeck was continuing to "rattle the traps of suburbia and to find in the family skeleton small bones of contention—lost jackets, loud snoring, and 'illegal possession of junk food.' . . . Most of this is gently recycled from her syndicated columns but it's reasonably organized, quite fluent, and fresh enough to hook the hundred thousands who found *The Grass Is Always Greener* up their alley."

Her friend and AAHC (American Academy of Humor

Columnists) associate Art Buchwald wrote a fun review of *Cherries.*

"Before I get down to the business of reviewing Erma Bombeck's latest book," he began, "I think I have to make one thing perfectly clear: I know the author personally. We even had a little thing going between us at a Holiday Inn on the outskirts of Gary, Indiana, several years ago when we were both reading *Passages* and having our midlife crises at the same time."

And then Buchwald described Erma, as he saw her. "Despite what you see on television, which distorts the human face and figure, Erma is a tall, long-legged, beautiful natural blonde with Ivory soap skin, ruby-red pouting lips, Maidenform body, a waist that could easily belong to Alicia Markova, and hands that have never touched dishwater."

After portraying her as a combination of Rita Hayworth, Elizabeth Taylor, Julie Andrews, and Princess Grace of Monaco, Buchwald continued: "For years Erma Bombeck was thought of as nothing but a sex object." Then she started writing a column of humor, and "suddenly people realized there was a lot more to Erma Bombeck than being a poster in every Air Force ready room, every college dormitory, and every foxhole in the First Marine Division."

And, "She became the Betty Friedan of the Women's Humor Movement. Now, little girls all over America, when asked what they want to be when they grow up, reply, 'Erma Bombeck.' "

After all that preliminary vintage Buchwald, he got down to the nitty-gritty. "In this book, Erma gives us a sampling of her work. The trick is to see if you can read a paragraph without laughing out loud. I can't, and I don't laugh easily, particularly when I'm reading a competitor who is taking food out of my children's mouths."

Even if she felt she was standing behind Bill Russell in

the parade of life, Bombeck was a household name after the appearance and instant acceptance of her fifth book.

What to Do to Top Total Success

And, naturally, now was the time for an encore, an opus to top all her other opera, a joke to cap the latest jest. In Bombeck's case, the capper came in the form of a satire on self-help tomes, a long parody or spoof on books that tell one how to "deal" with oneself.

Thus, *Aunt Erma's Cope Book,* published in 1979.

The theme of the book is, of course, an extension of a subject she satirized many times in her newspaper columns. For example, the column discussed in Chapter Two is a typical parody. In the case of the self-help book, obviously, the target is already there, full-blown and inviting assault.

To organize the various satires or parodies cohesively, Bombeck ties together the various burlesques on bestsellers with a kind of story line. The narrator, a self-proclaimed "perfect woman," makes a kind of exploration tour through sixty-two self-help books, sampling all kinds of fads and ploys to try to understand and improve herself.

The odyssey begins not with the conclusion of the Trojan Wars, but when her husband enters his "metallic age: silver hair, gold teeth, and lead bottom." The heroine finds that her children are dying not to leave the nest, but to have *her* leave the nest.

"You feel used up, unfulfilled, unappreciated. Your life is in the Twilight Zone. And you live in fear. Fear that your children are writing a sequel to *Mommie Dearest*. Fear of dying after you've just eaten a crummy tasteless salad with a low-calorie dressing. Fear of going to a partner-swapping party and no one wants to swap with you."

So says her friend Nancy to her.

And Bombeck's heroine steps through the looking glass and finds a land that does not exist except in the jingling cash registers of bookstores across the face of America, a land invented to please the fancies and fantasies of people with nothing to worry about who want to feel guilty.

On to the laundry list of books, most of them instantly recognizable by a turn of phrase: *Looking for Mr. Goodbody; Is There a Draft in Your Open Marriage?; Fear of Buying; The Neurosis Cookbook; Inner Walking; Body English Spoken Here; Living Cheap; Packages (Passages);* and so on.

In each instance, as she tries to follow the advice of one of the books, she is thwarted by the members of her family: Jaws II, her son, who eats more and more each day and gets hungrier and hungrier; her daughter in from college; or her husband, who still asks "Anybody home?" as he stares directly at her.

Nevertheless, at the book's end, Bombeck's heroine claims to have "come to grips with midlife, found inner peace, fought outer flab, interpreted my fantasies, examined my motive for buying, dissected my marriage, charted my astrological stars, and become my best *and only* friend. I have brought order to my life, meditated, given up guilt, adjusted to the new morality, and spent every living hour understanding me, interpreting me, and loving me—and you know what? I'm bored to death with me. If I never have another word about me it will be too soon."

Bombeck's point is that you don't find happiness if you seek it deliberately and painstakingly; it finds you.

"After reading sixty-two books and articles on how to deal with oneself, I realized something was missing. A sense of humor. I cannot believe that people look into the mirror that reflects their actions and behavior and keep a straight face."

Parody and burlesque are tricky subjects when offered

to the public through any of the entertainment media. In the theater, the axiom that has been many times proved goes, "Satire is what closes on Saturday night." Satirical articles in newspapers and magazines are frequently misunderstood. Irony baffles most recipients. Even the comic pages have trouble with satire: "Li'l Abner" died after years of very pointed spoof. "Doonesbury" is popular now, but gets into periodic trouble. "Pogo" never made big money for its creator.

But Bombeck did it and did it big with *Aunt Erma's Cope Book*. She even got good reviews, and was good enough even to be parodied in the *New York Times*! Imagine that, a parody of a parody.

The *New York Times Book Review* assigned Caroline Seebohm to handle the book. "In each chapter," she wrote, "[Bombeck] exposes herself to the various home therapies (Sensual Needlepoint, Inner Jogging, Colorcoding Your Leftovers) promoted in such catchily titled books as *The Sub-Total Woman* . . . But of course our Erma doesn't get self-improved at all, and at the end finds her biorhythms still out of sync. When she gives up on the literature of self-help, she suffers withdrawal symptoms: sweaty palms and dry throat. These are good jokes.

"There are some less good jokes in passages (or packages) of dialogue and anecdotes that permit transitions between the good jokes. It's all very light indeed and you can read it in one sitting, while you wait for your waxy yellow buildup to dry."

Dennis Petticoffer, of Pasadena, reviewed the book for *Library Journal*: "Few contemporary humorists are more popular or prolific than housewife, mother, and nationally syndicated columnist Erma Bombeck. *Aunt Erma's Cope Book* satirizes self-help advocates and so-called friends whose candor and concern provoke them to hand out free advice. Inevitably their tips turn out to be more burdening than helpful . . . Bolstered by an underlying 'be thyself' philosophy and the 'medicine' of laughter, Erma's tortured (tongue-in-cheek) testimonials may actually be more therapeutic than most serious self-help books. The lighthearted volume is sure to be in demand.''

Nevertheless there was some confusion among the reviewers. A Los Angeles newspaper critic reacted: "[*Aunt Erma's Cope Book*] is not nearly as funny as *Life Is Always Greener over the Septic Tank. . . .*'' (Presumably the critic meant *The Grass* rather than *Life*.) Simultaneously, another newspaper critic in Cincinnati wrote: "The *Cope Book* is more enjoyable than *If Life Is a Bowl of Cherries—What Am I Doing in the Pits*, and you don't have to be particularly interested in the self-help fads to appreciate her humor.''

But most of the reviews were pluses. "The woman with the dry wit and shaky id, Erma Bombeck, generates some laughs of her own in this parody of the self-help fad in her *Cope Book*, subtitled 'How to Get from Monday to Friday in 12 Days.' ''

"First, a word about Erma Bombeck,'' another newspaper reviewer wrote. "Not enough can be said about this woman. A poet laureate of suburbia, she single-handedly has brought to the dumped-upon states of housewifery and motherhood what they need most—perspective, which is to say, a realization of *commedia dell'arte*. For that alone, she deserves sainthood.''

Another wrote: "Erma Bombeck is an important national resource, like coal and soft toilet paper. One day her face will be on a stamp—under the heading, 'Humorist, author, and think-thin activist.'

"Until the day when she gets the serious recognition she deserves, it's up to her readers to give her the recognition she has earned.''

One of the highest accolades that can be given any creative person is imitation; the second-highest is parody or burlesque. One must be doing things right to be satirized.

On June 8, 1980, Bombeck, the newly crowned Queen of Parody, was in turn parodied by "Richard Smith" in the *New York Times Book Review*.

Under the title "Uncle Richard's Cope Book," the piece said, in part:

"It all began a year ago. I'd been feeling inferior ever since my overachieving neighbor, Murray Porsche, told me that his nine-year-old son, whose voice had changed, had been given the lead in the year's fourth grade production of *Lohengrin*. My son, ever the disappointment, would understudy the swan."

(Richard gets a self-help book, studies it, and tries to improve his life.)

"I started with honesty. When my neighbor showed me his baby's snapshot, instead of forcing a smile, I said the kid resembled a mango. . . .

"I avoided orgasms, especially those that occur during tennis. . . .

"I grew more aggressive and cleaned a fish—while it was still swimming.

"And no more Mister Nice Guy. At my daughter's wedding, I had a cash bar.

"I know I'm not yet perfect. . . . But I'm on the right track. Just yesterday, in a fit of assertiveness, I refused to take out the garbage, then set fire to my son's homework, and, on the way to work, socked a vegetarian."

Where will it all end?

Chapter 8

Alter Erma

The Girl in the Gucci Yellow Hard Hat

No one can be "on" all the time, making jokes, keeping her fans in stitches of laughter, pouring out humor endlessly. Everyone, including the irresistible Bombeck, must exercise a more serious, more personal, more straight side.

Bombeck's alter ego is a logical extension of her humorous self.

"People write me and say, 'Gee, you could do so much good if you'd write about such and such,' " Bombeck told a magazine writer some years ago.

"I couldn't do any good at all because I'd love my audience. I don't have a message. I write to make myself feel better. I started the column out of sheer boredom and one reason my column is read is that people want relief from the grimness they find in the rest of the paper. They want to laugh at something."

That was in 1971. Since that time, Bombeck's attitude has changed somewhat, although the main force of her argument—that she wants to make people laugh at the grimness around them—remains. But she has widened the target of her satire.

She still describes herself as "a pair of white socks in

a pantyhose world," and sets limits on her public utterances so that she hardly ever makes pronouncements on "anything more controversial than static cling," as *People* magazine puts it.

When she started, she confined herself strictly to ironing boards, kids, husbands, and household situations. But she was also suspicious of activists, political and social. They were targets for satirical thrusts. She once called hard-core women's libbers "roller derby dropouts and Russian pole-vaulting types."

But since she started writing, much has happened to the American housewife. Now, sixteen years later, the housewife for whom she wrote then and for whom she writes now has changed.

"I'm writing for a different woman now," she says. "She's not standing behind the picture window anymore. She's taken the bus and gone into town.

"My life has been changed by the same things that have changed all women. My horizons are broader—not just kids, tuna recipes, and crabgrass—and so are the readers' horizons."

In fact, fellow columnist Ellen Goodman senses a change in Bombeck's attitude over the years. "Her children are gone," Goodman notes. "She and her husband are left alone. There's an edge to her column that wasn't there before."

Bombeck says that she prefers "playing it down the middle," to going all the way into a more serious milieu. She means that she is for the Equal Rights Amendment, but does not belong to the National Organization for Women.

She resents the fact that the leaders of the so-called women's rights movement never sought to enlist the services of the housewife in their battle for equality.

Her first impression of a women's rights leader was a memorable one. "When Betty Friedan came to our town in the mid-60s and spoke we roared when she made some comments about how some [television] commercials put women down—captains in the toilet tank and that sort of thing.

"Friedan was furious when we laughed," she chuckles. " 'This isn't funny,' she shouted, 'this is serious.' Of course, it *was* funny to us housewives. The problem with the women's movement is that it's been too elitist."

Bombeck means that the leaders of the movement have usually been women who have never been housewives, and who have never had children, and some of whom have never even been married. The "war" is, or was, being waged by women who did not really understand the people they were trying to direct into combat.

"One day in a leading magazine, I saw a story called 'Today's Woman on the Go,' " Bombeck says. "At the top of the article was a picture of a well-stacked blonde at a construction site with a group of men around her while she read blueprints to them. I noted her shoes were co-ordinated with her Gucci yellow hard hat.

"The second picture showed her in a pair of flowing pajamas standing over a stove stirring her filet-mignon helper (recipe on page 36) while her husband tossed the salad and her children lovingly set the table. It made me want to spit up."

She believes in the women's liberation movement, and always did, but, she adds with a slightly malicious gleam in the eye, "They picked out the American housewife as the battleground for the whole movement, but they didn't invite us to the war. I would personally like to wring the neck of whoever invented that phrase 'just a housewife' because, basically, that's what I still am."

In addition, Bombeck says, "No one ever asked me to make a stand. Which I think is fairly typical. We house-wives were the last to be asked what we wanted. That's probably why the amendment is in trouble today. Finally the feminists are coming to us and saying, 'We can't do it without you.' "

But where were they when the battle lines were being drawn?

"When did a woman selling orange slices in the dime store become more impressive than a woman who did a darned good job raising three kids for twenty years?" Bombeck asks with some asperity.

Yet she still says that even if she does have opinions on just about everything in Washington and all around the world, she, Bombeck, is not writing about them in her daily columns. She avoids all types of controversy in her three-times-a-week stint, and admits that whenever she has any doubts about a subject, she'll leave it out and ignore it.

Sometimes it's difficult to keep the column clean—the current mores in America being what they are—but she thinks there's nothing in her writing that she wouldn't want her children to read.

"I am antiabortion," she admits. "But I don't want to inflict my beliefs on other people. I'll do it privately, but I won't do it in a column. I'll inflict my kids, my husband, my marriage, my home, domestic situations—anything I think is going to make them laugh that day. But not serious things.

"[These things are] not for the column or the books," she says. "Lots of subjects can't be handled humorously. I stick close to home—I'm still exploiting my children, husband, and family life. I know where my domain is."

But she doesn't really stick all that close to home in a physical, non-column sense. She still travels hundreds of miles on speaking tours in favor of ERA ratification. She also solicits local support for battered wives and children in Arizona. And she serves on the boards of the Arizona Kidney Foundation and other local groups.

And she admits to a change in attitude from her earlier

days. "I've undergone a transition. I'm into new things. I'm writing from a different vantage point now, not dealing with motherhood constantly. The status of women has broadened my horizons. It's been great for me."

Whatever Happened to Justa Housewife?

Bombeck is most serious in her gripe, as already noted, about the use of the put-down phrase "Are you Justa Housewife?"

Early in 1978, she was invited to deliver a speech at a seminar cosponsored by the *Ladies Home Journal* and Kentucky Fried Chicken. The meeting was titled: "Homemaker: Career in Transition." It was there that Bombeck delivered a speech on being "Justa Housewife." Excerpts from the text were later printed in the February 1978 issue of the *Journal*. In the article Bombeck's thoughts on being "just a housewife" are spelled out:

She introduces her piece by pointing out that for almost thirteen years she has been writing about the typical American housewife, exposing her frailties, her frustrations, and her loneliness.

She goes on to point out that the only way to improve the housewife's position is to change it by the proper legislation.

Then, with typical Bombeck agility, she shifts from persuasion to humor, and lists the so-called bills:
• To raise the driving age of a child to 35.
• To lower the age of menopause to 12.
• To allow a mother to abandon a child in a restroom after he has kicked the back of his mother's seat for 300 miles without stopping.

Bombeck then describes the stereotype housewife of those days. She was a lousy driver. She spent all her time at the ironing board. She appeared in commercials talking about her kids' cavities, her washing machine, and her irregularity.

A stereotype in every sense, Bombeck notes, called by a coined nickname—Justa Housewife.

She follows up her description of Justa Housewife with a typical scene in the kitchen one morning: one child pulling out the dirty laundry trying to find something to wear; another asking for a costume for a school play—"he was a participle," Bombeck explains; the bank calling to say there were insufficient funds to cover her check to the paper boy; the dog with catsup on its paws; her husband kicking up a fuss about taking his lunch to work in a Seven Dwarfs box.

And then, in the 1960s, Bombeck recalls, everything changed. Authorities popped up everywhere, telling exactly what the housewife wanted and needed to fulfill herself. And while the experts argued, the housewife who was the rope in the tug of war never seemed to be able to do anything right.

To complain, Bombeck points out, made her neurotic; but not to complain made her stupid. To stay at home with her children made her boring and smothering; but to go out and work made her selfish. To discuss the future made her husband depressed; but to discuss the past made her depressed.

Things were changing. Bombeck illustrates the change by describing a situation in her own home. She had hired a woman to babysit for her children while she did volunteer work in a nursery. At the nursery were the kids the babysitter had dropped off in the morning so she could babysit for Bombeck!

And then, of course, came the beginning of the women's liberation movement.

Bombeck thinks it was the most exciting thing ever to happen to American women. Every woman in the country was touched by it one way or another. To many, it was what they had always hoped and prayed for: a ticket out of the kitchen.

She describes a wrenching change that suddenly transformed suburbia. All the women in her own neighborhood were gone, leaving notes to the milkman, leaving dry cleaning inside the door, leaving keys under the doormat.

Justa Housewife didn't live there anymore.

But Justa Housewife still exists, Bombeck says. She imagines herself sitting down at her typewriter to do a story on a woman who announces excitedly that she has just got a new job.

It is called being a housewife and mother. And when someone asks her how she got the job—that is, did she know someone? did she take the right courses? or did she just happen to be there at the right time?—the answer comes as a surprise.

"I qualified," she answers them, and she smiles.

And Bombeck's tag line reads: "And that's all any of us wants."

The Day the Volunteers All Quit

Bombeck has always been an advocate of volunteerism. It is one of the sad things about equal rights for women that makes the volunteer almost an anachronism in modern society. One of the humorist's more serious columns deals with her idea of the end of volunteerism.

She relates a dream she has had, a dream that the volunteers in America, sad and depressed over the lack of compassion in the country, have set sail for another world, like Columbus so long ago.

Bombeck finds herself standing on the pier, waving to a boatload of them as they vanish into the distance.

It is the end of the world of volunteerism as it is known today, she realizes. No more creamed chicken. No more phone committees. No more Disease of the Month. No more saving old egg cartons. No more running around and getting out the vote. No more bake sales, playground duty, and three-hour meetings.

Well, she thinks vindictively, it is their own fault. They are all a bunch of do-gooders. If they didn't want to volunteer, all they had to do was say no. That would have spared them a great deal of time and trouble. Anyway, who needs them?

Her dream takes her to a hospital. It is absolutely empty. The rooms have no donated books, no flowers given by volunteers. There are no visiting nurses, no clowns acting in the children's wings, no laughter, no one to greet her cheerfully at the desk.

The Home for the Aged is deadly quiet. At the Home for the Blind, the blind listen for the voice that never speaks. The infirm are sitting in chairs that do not move. Food rests on trays that will never be carried to the hungry.

Social agencies cannot implement their programs of recreation, drug control, scouting, Big Sisters, YW, YM, the retarded, the crippled, the lonely, the abandoned.

In the health agencies there are signs hung up in the window: "Canceled Due to Lack of Interest: cures for cancer, muscular dystrophy, birth defects, multiple sclerosis, emphysema, sickle cell anemia, kidney disorders, heart disease, etc."

The schools are strangely quiet, she finds, with no field trips using volunteer aids on the playground or in the classrooms.

In the churches, flowers wither and die. In day nurseries children lift their arms, but there is no one to hold them. Alcoholics cry out in despair, but no one answers. The poor have no recourse for health care or legal aid.

Symphony Hall is dark and will remain that way. So are the museums built and stocked by volunteers with art treasures and artifacts.

"I fought in my sleep to regain a glimpse of the ship of volunteers just one more time," Bombeck concludes. "It was to be my last glimpse of civilization . . . as we were meant to be."

The Great American Pollution Centennial

In December 1978 *People* magazine decided to make use of Erma Bombeck's sense of commitment to one of the country's most vital problems: pollution. Introducing Bombeck's report, which appeared in the December 25 issue, the editors wrote:

"This magazine is not all celebs and glamour. We don't flinch from the hard news and thorny issues of the day. When a significant anniversary came to our attention recently, we sought out a journalist with a reputation for covering the tough ones. Reporter Erma Bombeck, who developed her investigative skills on Ohio's *Kettering-Oakwood Times* and the *Dayton Journal-Herald*, filed this report."

In the report on the centennial of U.S. pollution—its first hundred years in the U.S.—Bombeck establishes the tradition of the tongue-in-cheek Pollution Centennial:

"Do you honestly think L.A. was polluted in a day? It takes work to pollute a country. Hard work. We're talking about 3,615,122 square miles of land, 78,267 square miles of water, 12, 383 miles of coastline, and only 218 million people to do the job."

As mastermind of the Pollution Centennial, Bombeck's interviewee, Dan Taint, refuses at first to talk about the centennial.

"Everyone enjoys the results of pollution," he tells Bombeck, "but no one wanted to pitch in. It could have been such a great birthday party, a real fun year of dancing, playing, feasting, coughing. I wanted to stage a birthday party that America could be proud of."

Bombeck then quotes Taint as he lists the "gala events" he has planned for the centennial celebration:

"I was going to have 180 tankers sail into Boston Harbor, leaking oil. Arizona was going to dedicate a new nuclear plant. The Concorde had plans to buzz all the army hospitals in the United States and drop leaflets saying, 'We're doing our little bit for the centennial.'. . . I had a caravan of cars ready to leave Detroit in August with faulty emissions, drive to California, be recalled, and drive back again. Montana was going to open a new strip mine. In Florida there were plans for 50 crop dusters to spread insecticide over a 200-mile radius and make people sick."

In addition, Taint says, he was planning eight billion bumper stickers reading: TAKE A SMOKER TO LUNCH.

"Even schoolchildren were to be part of the celebration," Taint adds. "We were going to drop off one junked car per student in schoolyards all over the country, and let the kids go at them with bright paint."

Taint also mentions a plan in the dream stage—to have everyone turn in old stick deodorants and be given free aerosol cans in return.

"In New York," he tells Bombeck, "we were going to give prizes for the best calling-card design left on a hydrant by a large dog."

But Taint sadly tells Bombeck that the whole idea fell apart. What did in the centennial celebrations? "Apathy. Lack of vision."

Americans, Taint complains, aren't big thinkers. "They're penny-candy-wrapper droppers, beach litterers, hole-in-the-muffler supporters. When you stage a 100th anniversary, you have to think big. Oh, well, as Doris Day once said, 'Que Sierra, Sierra.' "

"That's 'Que sera, sera,' " Bombeck corrects him.

Taint promises Bombeck that "the bicentennial of pollution in 2078 is going to be a success if it kills us."

Humor? Yes. But the satire in this piece comes close to

being a serious attack on a major problem in America today.

The Night Tinker Bell Died

But more serious than pollution is another major problem of today's society: the crisis in confidence—self-confidence, confidence in one's fellow man, confidence in the country.

Bombeck isn't afraid to tackle that one, either. When *Newsweek* magazine asked her for her thoughts on the confidence crisis, Bombeck turned out for the magazine the column "Will America Regain Its Trust?" The piece was printed on November 19, 1979, and was later published in the January 1980 issue of *Current*.

"It hasn't happened yet," Bombeck begins, "but it's inevitable. One night, Sandy Duncan will lean over the footlights of a Broadway theater and in the childlike voice of Peter Pan, ask, 'Will everyone who believes in Tinker Bell clap your hands?' And the theater will resound in silence. The silence will record the last Bastille of blind faith in America."

That is the problem Bombeck worries a great deal about. She calls it trust, but actually what she is worrying about is more than trust; it is confidence, faith, reliance, promise, and a kind of justified hope.

And America has lost it.

"Who knows what triggered it?" she goes on. "Maybe it began when Washington introduced a new dance to the nation, the evasion shuffle. (One step forward, two steps back, swing around the truth, and change stories.) Whatever it was, the skepticism and mistrust filtered down into every part of our lives."

Then, she goes on, the disintegration began. National institutions that everyone had always believed in began to fall from favor:

"The U.S. Food and Drug Administration reported to-day that in testing research rats, red dye in lipstick was found to cause cancer."

But the people doubted the test. If the research rats were dying over red dye in lipstick, how come the same re-search rats that had been plied with booze, cigarettes, drugs, pollution, radiation, disease, and lipstick still out-numbered human beings?

Children, Bombeck continues, began to suspect the truth in statements their parents made; statements like "We'll talk about it tomorrow"; or "This is going to hurt me worse than it does you." Kids, Bombeck says, began to suspect Santa Claus, goodness over evil, patriotism, a hot breakfast, and the "myth" of marriage.

"We were all raised on trust," Bombeck notes. "It was considered one of the better virtues. But it lulled us into apathy and down the path of blind acceptance. It has become a luxury we can no longer afford."

Trust, she points out, led nine hundred Americans to drink cyanide for a man named Jones who had conned them into the jungles of Guyana. Trust faltered after a nuclear plant on Three Mile Island sprang a leak. Trust died when drivers found a Chevy engine in an Oldsmobile body.

"Out of this decade has emerged a new American who is questioning, skeptical, and challenging," writes Bom-beck. "If you invited him down the Yellow Brick Road, he'd want to know who the contractor was, what the stress factor is, and what is at the end of it before he sets foot on it."

She concludes:

"The question we face in the 1980s is not whom will Americans trust again, but, more important . . . why?"

Just a Normal Nonviolent American Mother

In line with her transition into a more militant women's

rights activist, Bombeck traveled to Salt Lake City in May 1980 to address the National Student Nurses' Association convention.

She arrived at a city which was in the middle of a political-religious controversy stirred up by the Equal Rights Amendment. Sonia Johnson, a feminist Mormon, had been excommunicated by church elders because of her support of the amendment.

Without once looking back, Bombeck waded into the controversy and expressed her dissatisfaction with the actions of the elders. She expressed sympathy for any woman caught up on a religious battlefield in a crossfire of wills. "I'm gratified," she told her audience, "that I don't have to choose between God and my conscience."

She also said that the Mormon's contention that ERA would endanger the family as an institution was "illogical."

"If there were a formula for having a wonderful family," she told them, "and that formula said 'get rid of ERA,' I'd probably be first in line. But I don't think you can use the ERA as a dumping ground for all the problems the family is having."

She was not totally serious in all her utterances. For example, she used her own brand of humor to describe herself and her family:

"I would classify myself," she told them from the podium, "as a nonviolent mother of three unplanned children. I've been married to the same man for thirty-one years, with whom I've never had a meaningful conversation in my entire life.

"I iron by demand, have a daughter who is twenty-six years old and has no curiosity as to how to turn on a stove. And I have two sons who make Cain and Abel look like Donny and Marie Osmond."

And then she zeroed in on the equal rights controversy generally.

"We've got to get sex out of the gutter and back into the Constitution where it belongs," she said. "The ERA cause—'equality of rights under the law'—may be the most misunderstood words since 'one size fits all.' "

And she once again stated her main gripe with the women's liberation movement:

"I liken the ERA to a war in which they forgot to invite the housewives. I volunteered. No one approached me and said, 'Bombeck, get out and lend your name to this thing.' "

And she then turned to the women in her audience of National Student Nurses' Association members: "You are probably the last of the women's groups to demand your rights."

Bombeck got good coverage for her Utah appearance, both in *People* magazine and in the newspapers. *People* reporter Frank W. Martin pointed out that Bombeck is not the only person trying to hew out a place for herself among the many unorganized and disunited housewives in the country.

"Though they are dissimilar in most respects," he wrote, "[Bombeck] knows that a major competitor in her quest for the support of the silent majority is anti-ERA militant Phyllis Schlafly."

Asked if she would debate with Schlafly, Bombeck retorted: "You can't talk to Phyllis on a one-to-one basis. She does a monologue on you. She does a good job of selling herself and has a strong power base. If I left this earth tomorrow, there would be a few million to take my place. If the same thing happened to Phyllis, I can't think of a replacement."

Think that remark over. The barbs are hidden, but they do draw blood.

When Bombeck Speaks, People Listen

Early in the administration of President Jimmy Carter,

Erma Bombeck was appointed a member of the President's Advisory Committee for Women. At first she was inclined to play down her own importance on the committee. "Really," she told one reporter, "I'm picked for the public appearance and show-business part of things."

Nevertheless, along with other people like Lena Epps Brooker, Suzanne Monson, Mayor Isabella Cannon, and Lynda Bird Robb, Bombeck continued to support the committee after it was almost torn apart completely when President Carter dismissed its first chairman, Bella S. Abzug.

Bombeck was one of only fifteen committee members who remained after twenty-five of the forty resigned in protest over the President's move. Most of the resigners thought that the committee had lost its effectiveness.

Not all her colleagues think she's simply there for glamour reasons. "Bombeck is too shy to admit that she's the one who told the committee to concentrate on the ERA," says Esther Landa, former head of the National Council of Jewish Women. "When she has something to say, people listen."

Bombeck once told a reporter for the *New York Times* that she attends the committee meetings because she gets an insight into women, and sees the frustration. "That's what I write about, frustration."

But Bombeck also has another motivation.

"I'm doing it for my kids," she says. "It will be important to them. It's also a great feeling to be part of history. I wish that they could put this on my tombstone: 'She got Missouri for the ERA.' "

Campaigning for Equal Laughs

Bombeck's speaking tours in favor of the Equal Rights Amendment have already taken her to a number of states.

In January 1979 she and Liz Carpenter, a Texas Democrat and former press secretary for Lady Bird Johnson, were in North Carolina trying to persuade the voters to ratify the ERA.

She played nice girl to Carpenter's tough girl in their joint appearances. When Carpenter would flail away in a good hardsell stance, Bombeck lightened the thrusts with typical humorous comments.

She described herself as a "nice girl out of the utility room who is used to sorting socks." She told her listeners that they had nothing to fear from the ERA.

"Those words, Equal Rights Amendment," she said, "are the most misunderstood words since 'one size fits all.' "

Later on in Iowa, in June 1980, the dynamic duo were once again paired in the nice girl/tough girl team approach.

"Has everyone seen the dress?" Bombeck asked the crowd. "I just can't suck in my stomach for an hour and a half. For those of you who didn't see me walk in, I'm just like Marlo Thomas."

During her talk she inserted a parody of the presidential campaign which was being fought at the time, satirizing Ronald Reagan, Jimmy Carter, and John Anderson and their platforms.

"This is the Bombeck-Carpenter initial Presidential Fundraiser and Tupperware Party," she said, to rally the troops. "We believe the country is ready for a woman in the White House who doesn't do windows or floors."

She went on to explain the platform they had dreamed up, and the catch-phrases they had written to get press coverage and encourage protest marches.

"We favor a child on every pot.

"You have nothing to fear but cellulite.

"Has Ronald Reagan ever gone into maternity clothes at two weeks? Has Jimmy Carter ever lusted for an after-five dress and gotten a flannel nightgown? Has John Anderson ever taken a knot out of a shoestring with his teeth that a kid has wet on all day long?"

She also pointed out that the typical, one-hundred percent pure housewife hardly exists anymore. The increase in the number of working mothers, she said, now allowed her to change her jokes to reflect the difference.

For example, now she can write about a child who telephones to drag his mother out of a high-level business conference to ask her whether or not he can share a bottle of Pepsi with his brother.

Or, she can write about a child who calls up to announce he has been in a fight, is bleeding, and is lying on a sofa that no one has as yet Scotchgarded; what should he do?

But, she pointed out, even though she believes in the ERA and stumps around the country in favor of it, she feels that her column is not a place to bring up the issue.

"They are two separate things," she explains, meaning her political stumping and her writing.

The ERA, she believes, is a good thing for the country because the United States was "founded on compassionate laws for everyone."

Gourmet Dishes, That's What's Cooking!

Bombeck helps out local causes as well as national ones. For example, in Phoenix in February 1981 she participated in a black-tie dinner-dance at $75 a head to raise money for the March of Dimes' fight against birth defects.

She was one of eleven local celebrities in a cook-off competition, to be judged by a panel including *New York Times* gourmet editor Craig Claiborne.

Amanda Blake, "Gunsmoke's" Miss Kitty, and Hollywood actress Jane Wyatt headed a roster of other celebrities who assisted the cooks.

Bombeck was one of the cooks. "That rumor that I can't cook is just a big, ugly myth," she told Dorothee Polson of the *Arizona Republic.* "I've heard those stories, that all I can make is rock soup; that punishment for my children was being sent to bed *with* dinner."

She shook her head. "Not true. Cooking is my life. I even take gourmet cooking classes."

Bombeck then told the columnist how she defined gourmet dishes. "That's recipes written with words you can't understand, calling for ingredients you can't get."

She even told her she planned to wear an "obscene apron" while she cooked, and would submit three recipes: cucumber soup, pork with beer, and marinated mushrooms Bombeck.

The marinated mushrooms dish was definitely a gourmet recipe. "Directions say to wash the mushrooms in acidulated water. I don't know what that is, so I use tap water."

Bombeck explained how she had got into the world of cooking. "I started cooking because of my three children. I had to feed them." She used her own system, which she designated the "trough" system.

"I cooked a lot of macaroni and cheese or anything that would fatten them up. The children are grown and gone now, although none is married." She let that statement hang as a non sequitur.

"Now I am more selective about what I cook. For just my husband and myself I serve fewer courses, less meat, less of all food. I use the wok more, more vegetables, no desserts."

For entertaining, she said she found the challenge diverting. "My dinner parties are casual, loose. And I start with an advantage: People think I can't cook, so they don't expect much. They come with a sense of humor and are pleasantly surprised with just a one-dish meal and good rolls."

About the upcoming cook-off she was somewhat sanguine. "Even though gala guests will be allowed to talk with us while we're cooking, I don't anticipate being nervous. Even if I cut myself, I'll keep signing autographs, probably with my own blood."

Asked by the *Arizona Republic*'s Polson what her husband thinks about her cooking, Bombeck retorted: "What does he know?"

Chapter 9

Here's Erma!

A Cornier Doris Day

The secret of Erma Bombeck's universal appeal, says one writer, is twofold: (1) her relentless, studious averageness; and (2) her basic sense of humor. The "studious averageness" is the key phrase to describe Bombeck's basic appeal. By being average, Erma Bombeck is following in the line of the greatest of American humorists.

And at the same time, even though she is linked by tradition to the roots of American humor, as we have seen, Bombeck has created a new kind of humor—the suburban supermarket/utility room/kitchen humor of today. It is different from Jean Kerr's more sophisticated version of the career woman-housewife; or from that of the other humorists we have surveyed.

"It's difficult to believe that Erma is not something entirely new in the field of American humor," says Betty Dunn in a *Life* magazine article. "Neither hayseed nor urban, never 'in,' not a black humorist, not droll or sophisticated—at her unselfconscious best, Erma's is the voice of the hearty school chum who'd let you take a spin on her bike anytime."

Herbert Mitgang observes: "Erma Bombeck never writes

about the neutron bomb, the gross national product, Euro-communism, the West Bank of the Jordon, President Carter's effectiveness, or all the tea in China.

"Instead, her meat-and-potatoes, fast-food themes center on her children, husband, cars, neighbors, television watching, the laundry and supermarket, her mother, honeymoons, and hair curlers. She's a cornier Doris Day, a cleaner Maud, and your Aunt Tillie on her first trip to Paris."

"About one hundred and ten percent of what I write is from real experience," Bombeck says. "All I do is watch the human condition and write it down. It's like stealing. Family vacations, for instance, provide wonderful material. You know the child who kicks the back of the car seat for four hundred miles and who chants for another two hundred and fifty: 'He's looking at me again. Make him stop.' That child is a terrific subject, and I just have to polish the dialogue."

In fact, the humor is always around her—in the supermarket, with its wall-to-wall terrain of name brands; in the suburb with its weddings and funerals, its hair appointments; in the television set with its cowboys and private eyes and sex symbols. Erma Bombeck has always been exactly where most people live a good part of the time.

"I think a lot when I iron," Bombeck confesses. "It's peaceful, quiet, I think of a phrase or something and run away and write it down. The tinier the little thing is the more I like it. Robert Benchley topics, I call them. Little bitty things. I get carried away with the absurdity of a situation.

"My son came home from a basketball game one night, last winter," she goes on. "I had made him wear boots and when I asked him if he'd had a good time, he said, 'I was humiliated. Nobody was wearing boots!' That hit me all of a sudden. I thought, 'My God, I'm the only mother in the United States of America making her son wear boots!'

"I could picture the whole scene in the gymnasium, the screaming crowd, the hush that fell when he walked in. Then a spotlight following him to his seat. Then somebody chanting: 'He is darling, he is cute; he is wearing baby boots!'

"Then you get carried away even farther—to downtown, going by a store window full of boots, you think: 'Are you crazy? You'll starve to death! No one will buy them!' "

With a little smile, Erma concludes: "I like to get into a little subject like that and just run with it."

Although most columns in the newspaper, especially those on the women's pages (now usually called "lifestyle pages"), contain advice for the housewife—how to get a boyfriend, how to repair appliances, how to baste both chickens and hems, how to stretch the food dollar, how to cope with sciatica, and so on—Bombeck never rises to these occasions.

Instead, she may dream up ten arguments to throw at a kid who wants to bring home a bull snake from vacation. (A snake won't go on a leash with you to the supermarket, and will be doomed to a monk's existence alone in a Coke bottle—what if the snake wanted to date and eventually have a family?) Or she might discuss a neighbor's distress over wife-swapping. (No one will trade with her.) Or she might attack the convention of wearing name tags at conventions and school gatherings, since she finds it hard to socialize with people who spend thirty minutes or so talking to her left bosom.

"Writing isn't always . . . easy, of course," she says. "There are some subjects that just will not work. When I roll the paper into the typewriter, I feel they should, but when nothing happens, I can get snow blindness from staring at the blank sheet.

"I've worked on some pieces for two days, and finally I look in the mirror and say, 'Why don't you face up to the fact that it's not going to work?' Then I get hysterical, cry a little, and say, 'You're absolutely right. Throw the thing away.'

"That's when I'll do anything, if my deadline allows it, to avoid the typewriter. I make necklaces out of paper clips; they reach down to my knees. I alphabetize my bills. I call up people my husband knew in the army. I make out Christmas card lists in July. I cook. I even clean my oven. That's the absolute last straw, but I have been known to do it."

The Bosom That Turned into a Shoulder

At one time, Bombeck considered herself a "typical housewife," but eventually she found that there is really no such thing, and that she isn't one, either.

"When you think in terms of the typical housewife, you think of someone who stays at home, raises children, goes to the market, cleans her own house, does some volunteer work, tends to her husband's needs—that sort of thing exclusively."

And, as an aside:

"I love that term 'working housewife.' It's so *redundant!*"

But, of course, the "typical houswife" actually becomes the target of Bombeck's prose. She is Erma's Justa Housewife, the "little person" she always writes about.

"God knows I have laughed at her frustrations. I have dissected her and picked her apart. I have done everything to her you can imagine. . . . But she doesn't feel put down by it, she doesn't feel I am making fun of her, she is able to laugh at herself.

"If I get away with it, it's probably because I am basically one of them, in spite of the current negative image of such a person."

Bombeck confesses that she writes humor not only to make people laugh, but also to help them feel better about themselves. She says she wants them to feel that they are not coming out of left field somewhere, are not weird, and are not unique.

"So you scream at your kids and get varicose veins of the neck. I mean, you're in good company, lady. You're keeping step with everybody else. We *all* feel that way."

Although most columnists and professional writers slant their material for a particular audience, Bombeck says she does not. "I write for me. I always have. There was a time when a women's column was confined to tuna casseroles. Now I can take off on anything."

Well, almost everything.

"I can't go over the brink and talk about too many things that border on the racy," she says. "Boy, I get letters! Once I used the word 'bathroom' and I got a letter from a woman editor of a little paper in Pennsylvania. If I used that word again, she said, she'd have to drop the column.

"For the first time I sat down and wrote a letter to the editor, trying to explain, being a mother is like being a doctor. Words like 'bathroom,' 'diarrhea'—you just rip 'em off.

"I'm always getting mail from people who think I'm sacrilegious. My son Andy is a picky eater. At home we say he's so picky he wouldn't eat at the Last Supper, but I can't use that in the column. I can write about the littlest thing and the mail comes pouring in. I did a column on large families once, saying maybe they weren't so bad. I'm still getting mail from ecology types on that. It's a bad year to be humorous about ecology."

In fact, in a column about name tags she mentioned people who spent thirty minutes talking to her "left bosom." Some newspapers changed the word *bosom* to *shoulder*.

"I *meant* bosom!" says Bombeck. "Other people get away with all kinds of things, but I can't even say 'bosom.' I don't even think 'bosom' is going too far."

The field of humor began narrowing some time ago, she points out. "That's a big problem in writing humor—so much sensitivity in so many areas. The sensitivity just gags you. Ohio is right next to Kentucky, and there's a sensitivity there, some friction. In a café in Dayton one time I overheard a waitress with a Kentucky accent talking to a customer and he asked her how she happened to be working there. 'Oh,' she said, 'I'm a GI bride!' Can you imagine? As if she was from Germany."

A great deal of her best humor turns out to be material from the past she has recollected in tranquillity.

"I get more satisfaction from my writing when I think back to when my children were babies. I recall a time in the supermarket when I told one of my toddlers to put a loaf of bread in Mama's cart.

"He said, 'I don't know which cart is ours.' I said, 'It has your baby brother in it. You can't miss it, hardly.'

"But, sure enough," Bombeck notes, "he did. I thought to myself, 'I have a real swift one on my hands.' "

And, "The fact is that most of the stuff that I find funniest is not what's happening now, but the things that happened back then, you know, in retrospect. Any pain has vanished, and now I've got the pure humor to draw from."

The Pain of Suburbia Is Everywhere

But suburbia to Erma Bombeck was always the most productive of places for humor. Although she never analyzed the reason for it, she says it is "probably because of the combination of people thrown together. Actually each suburb is a small autonomous community. Basically, each of them has the same economic level, the same religion, the same number of cars, the same Barbie dolls, the same everything. There is a sameness there that is absolutely incredible and therefore the subject of humor."

She has never devised any theory of humor, although she thinks of humor as the "other side of tragedy," as the Greeks did. When people in the suburbs laugh, they are laughing at some kind of pain.

"The pain in suburbia is everywhere," she says. "It is in the loneliness of women."

The suburbs are different from the city. "I've lived in both," she says. "There are some advantages to urban living. I was raised in sort of a downtown atmosphere. I got to meet more people, I was subjected to more situations, and I probably got a better education down there. I don't mean schoolwise.

"In contrast, suburbia is the great American dream. Two bathrooms and your own lawn. And it is a little slice of something that is yours and that you've worked for. I can see why people could be caught up by it. We were, too."

On the subject of humor, Bombeck has a number of things to say. For one thing, she has always thought that people take themselves too seriously.

"In fact, some people tell me, 'I don't understand what you're saying. I don't have a sense of humor.' I find that so hard to believe, because a sense of humor is such an easy thing to have. All you have to do is just throw caution to the wind and go with it."

Humor does a great deal for people. "It does everything. It could save your life. It really could, particularly when you're faced with a situation that you think you just cannot handle. We've had that in our marriage situations, where you think, 'Oh, my God, we're never going to survive this.' And then the humor comes back and says, 'Hey, we're going to be okay.' "

The reason people tend to take life too seriously, she

thinks, is that "if they take life seriously, they think that is going to be the answer for it, that they will control it. But this is not necessarily so."

And yet the business of writing is not at all times the best profession in the world.

"You can become very resentful of writing," Bombeck admits, "because it begins to own you. I sometimes think the thesaurus owns me. It seems to sit on the shelf and say, 'Erma, do you want to come and play?' Yet there's never been anything else I'd rather do. I never wanted to turn into a sitting-around-the-pool, painting-my-toenails kind of person."

She smiles. "What makes people laugh? It's an unknown thing. It's a happy marriage between a person who needs a laugh and someone who's got one to give."